How to use the

Unwritten
Rules of Success

to build your Dream Career

How to use the
Unwritten
Rules of Success
to build your Dream Career

Sean Terry, PhD

Library of Congress Control Number:		2011961840
ISBN:	Hardcover	978-1-4691-3117-7
	Softcover	978-1-4691-3116-0
	Ebook	978-1-4691-3118-4

To inquire about booking Dr. Terry for a professional development workshop or a presentation, please contact him at *unwrittenrulesterry@gmail.com*. Workshops can be of any length, and include a certificate of completion for participants.

This book was printed in the United States of America.

Cover design by Sarah Jones

To order additional copies of this book, contact:
Xlibris Corporation
1-888-795-4274
www.Xlibris.com
Orders@Xlibris.com
105335

Reviews

"The material offers the kind of practical suggestions and strategies that students of today can relate to—from helpful self-directed quizzes, to key unwritten rules designed to trigger thoughtful actions. As one strives for success in academic and professional endeavors, it is crucial to be deliberate in each step required. *"How to use the Unwritten Rules of Success to build your Dream Career"* provides a template sure to help in the journey."

—Mike Shirley PhD, Director, Breech School of Business.

"There is nothing out there exactly like this. It is a professional development text, but it goes farther than that in the following ways:

1. It provides real-life examples that people can immediately grasp in their own terms.
2. It gets right to the point with suggestions and quizzes that reinforce professional skills and behaviors.
3. It provides practice lessons to help the reader put the ideas of the text into action for their life.

—Andrew Weimer, Director of Leadership Programs,
Miami Florida

"*How to use the Unwritten Rules of Success to Build your Dream Career* is a very practical, easy-to-read guide that uncovers many strategies that will help students stand out rather than stick out in the 'real world'. Students will find it to be an invaluable professional development tool as they look forward to life after college".

—Jill Wiggins, Career Planning and Placement Director

"*Unwritten Rules* should be the handbook in every college student's backpack. Whether they are looking for a job, or continuing to graduate school, this book gives readers the edge by teaching them the standards of professionalism".

—Keely O'Sullivan, Financial Advisor Associate, Lyon Financial

"The Unwritten Rules are a launching pad to success. Those that read and apply the rules to their lives are headed for a prosperous frontier. Those that don't will be left behind."

—Kelsey Angle, Emergency Response Specialist Central Region, National Weather Service.

Contents

Preface

This book is designed for people who are about to enter the job market, are considering applying for graduate school, or are hoping to dramatically improve their work performance. It became clear in my early jobs and as a beginning master's student that the most important skills needed for success were not in the job description and were not taught in classes. It is very inefficient. We were often punished for not doing something that we were never told was a requirement for our job. These unwritten rules can often be more important than the written ones, so this book is designed to reveal them for you.

Despite doing good work in my early jobs and in college classes, I often saw fellow employees get promotions or other students getting graduate school offers by some mysterious process that I couldn't figure out. I started learning the ropes during my master's school training and used this newfound knowledge to successfully finish a PhD in record time. Now I am a university professor and have served as the Missouri director of education for National Geographic Society. I have spent the last twelve years observing and recording the things that separate successful people from the rest, and it is time to share that knowledge. How can you get that first great job, graduate fellowship, or promotion if you don't know all the rules? Now you can learn the rules before you apply. Using the experience of professional work, teaching, and student advising, I have prepared a list of sixteen qualities that can help you learn to follow the written and unwritten rules of success. Working on each of these categories will help you reach your professional goals. My student advisees learn these rules and then receive a personal interview based on their needs for the future. For many of them, this small investment in time has improved their chances for getting the first good job they want or getting paid to attend the graduate school of their choice. Based on a combination of job evaluation criteria and real-life experience, these skills will help you to achieve success in the real world.

These days, people often tell me that I am lucky. As a college professor, I get to travel extensively, spend time with my family, and have stimulating, rewarding job experiences. While I do admit to feeling blessed, the place where I find myself now is the result of a very concerted effort, not luck. Having an academic lifestyle and starting a family were part of a plan. Now that the basic plan has been realized, it takes continued effort to balance family time, work, and recreation in a sustainable way. Many people choose to blame an unsatisfying life on bad luck, while more successful people attribute their good fortune to working smarter and having an organized strategy. In my opinion, a lot of the "bad luck" in people's lives are the result of breaking the unwritten rules of success. I hope that the self-evaluation offered in this book will help give you an edge by showing you the rules the game of life and providing a method to practice them.

Acknowledgments

Every book is a product of hard work, and this one required the honest feedback from many sources. My original and most valued sources for life experience are my parents, Jim and Mary Terry. Their success in life was an inspiration to write this book and share the unwritten rules with others. My wife, Megan, has also served as an advisor for the entire work. She recommended further professional development training for me when I wasn't required to do it. Working on this new field was made much more fun and productive by sharing it with her. Finally, I would like to recognize the liberal arts tradition of Drury University. By embracing new teaching opportunities, especially ones that were outside my core academic discipline, I was able to develop new personal and professional directions. The result was a much deeper understanding of the subjects for this book.

Using the Book

It is recommended that you use the following methods to get the most out of the book.

1. Complete only one chapter per day in order to maximize retention of content. Read the chapter and complete the quiz. Then revisit the areas of the quiz where you had incorrect answers, and be sure you understand the reasoning behind the correct answer.
2. Write down the review items listed at the end of each chapter. Physically writing them down is the best way to commit them to memory and accept them as a new part of your professional life.
3. Pay special attention to the unwritten rules. These items are usually not found in applications or job descriptions, but they often make the difference between success and failure in real life. Try to incorporate these rules into daily personal and professional activities until they become habits.
4. Complete the self-evaluation at the end of each chapter and honestly rank your strengths and weaknesses. Then use the practice suggestions to help correct your weaknesses.
5. Complete the professional development worksheet at the end of the book. Work hard on any deficient areas, and you will see marked improvement in your own success.
6. Revisit the book at least once a year, as conditions change, or to reevaluate your professional progress. You will find that some sections become common practice, but different sections will become important as your situation changes and will require further practice.

Chapter 1

Make Your First Impression Count

My first job was as a busboy at the Riverside Inn in Ozark, Missouri. I was fifteen years old, and I rode my bike to the restaurant to inquire about the job. The secretary informed me that the owner was not in but would be back later. I filled out an application and remembered that I had been instructed by my father to be sure to see the owner face-to-face. Since he wasn't there, I sat down on a bench and waited. Three hours later, the owner arrived. I saw the secretary talk to him briefly, and then he came over to me. "Did you really wait on this bench for three hours to see me about a busboy job?" he asked. I said that I had. "Well, if your work ethic is as strong as your patience, you're hired," he said. Even though I didn't have any experience, I learned that persistence can sometimes be the strongest first-impression quality to help you win a job.

Modern society puts a lot of emphasis on first impressions. Whether it is a job application, interview, graduate fellowship application, or an important meeting, there are up to hundreds of applicants for each job opening, and a first impression leads to the initial screening. It may be the only chance you get to prove yourself. In order to pass this first test, there are several things that you must do.

Unwritten Rules of Chapter 1:

Make the First Impression Lead to a Second Impression

It is critical to do all the homework to be prepared for a job interview or scholarship application. The next time you fill out an application, be sure to find out all pertinent information, and then go further. Check their website to learn about the place. Ask the administrative assistant who will be evaluating the application. Ask what qualities are most desired for this position and ask if you can visit the job or school to get a feel for the place and talk to people. If you visit, you may get a chance to make a good first impression before your application is even submitted, and the interview itself will be a second impression. This effort will pay off for you no matter the result. Knowing more about the opportunity may lead you to understand that this is not the right place for you, and you may not need to submit an application (which can be costly, especially for graduate school, law school, or medical school applications). If it is the right place, you have now made a personal impression on someone in the office, and if at all possible, you have made a personal appearance to show your legitimate interest in the position and separated yourself from other applicants.

Always Be Punctual

The most important and first thing to remember for success is to be punctual. Get all paperwork completed correctly and turned in before the deadline. Most employers and college committees will throw away late applications, and many interviewers will not see you in person if you arrive late. Being punctual shows organizational ability and shows respect for the people you are trying to impress. The good news is that staying on time has never been easier. Reminder calendars on your computer and phone can help you keep on time.

Recommended times:

1. Get all required business paperwork in at least one week before the deadline. Schedule to have time to edit and finish and print out all college papers at least one day before the deadline. This allows for correction or resubmission if needed.
2. Arrive at all important face-to-face meetings in an office ten minutes before the meeting. Earlier than this makes you look too anxious, later cuts the timing too short.
3. If the meeting is a presentation, ask if the room will be available before the presentation, and arrive one hour early in order to set up

and practice your presentation before the other people arrive. If the same room is not available directly before your meeting, ask if there is a similar room with identical equipment where you can practice.

Look and Sound the Part

The second thing to do to make a good impression is to have the appropriate tone of voice and proper clothing for the event. In most situations, it is best to appear very calm, serious, and with a positive attitude. It is always appropriate to ask about dress code beforehand, but if you don't have this opportunity, casual dress will work in most modern situations.

Do Your Homework

The next thing to include is proper research. People are not impressed by a blabbermouth who goes on and on about things that are not related to the job at hand. They prefer a good listener, who is prepared to speak about the appropriate things related to this visit.

Questions you need to be able to answer to show that you are prepared are the following :

1. Why are you here, and how much do you really want this position?
2. How does your talent and experience make you a good candidate for this position? What valuable contribution will you bring with you?
3. What are the name and credentials of the person interviewing you?
4. What important information should you know about the job or graduate appointment you are applying for?

(These are important questions or concerns about the job that may be dealmakers or deal breakers for you.)

If you can't answer these questions, you need to do the research first and then apply. Another benefit of doing this research first is that it will sometimes show you that this is not the right position for you, so there is no need for you to take the time to apply.

Practice, Practice, Practice

Practice for interviews and presentations.

The final thing to do is to practice. Most colleges offer interview sessions at the career center. Some library centers have professional development workshops for free as well. If you are not currently a college student or do not have library or other job assistance services available, a friend or family member can help with this.

How to practice for an interview:

1. Write down the questions that your research has identified that are most likely to be asked, and practice answering them to a live person in the room.
2. Instruct your questioner to ask some odd questions as well to keep you on your toes.
3. If there will be a presentation, be sure to practice it in front of a live person to be sure that it fits the time schedule and to receive advice on how to improve the style and quality of the presentation. Prepare note cards, but don't prepare the whole text and read from it. The notes are for reference only; you should have a command of the material and make eye contact with the audience, not with your notebook.

First Impression Quiz

Answer the questions below. The answers can be found on the following pages.

	True	False

1. Punctuality is only important for business meetings. _____ _____

2. College professors don't care about punctuality, only the scores that you make on exams. _____ _____

3. Persistence can be more important than talent. _____ _____

4. Deadlines should always be strictly followed. _____ _____

5. I can wing it or BS my way through an interview. _____ _____

6. Content of your presentation is always more important than the appearance of your clothing and hair. _____ _____

7. I should bring extra formats for presentations. _____ _____

8. It is OK to print out documents the day they are due. _____ _____

9. It is acceptable to call an office for advice about a job. _____ _____

10. You should not drop names but should make a first impression on your own accomplishments only. _____ _____

Answers for the First Impression Quiz

1. False. Punctuality is always important. Where it is "the early bird gets the worm" or any number of other clichés, this is an extremely important habit to practice. Even if you are not the most talented candidate, if you are qualified and keep showing up on time, you will eventually get the job.

2. False. Punctuality at meetings or in the classroom shows respect to the person running the meeting and to everyone else who has taken the time to prepare the materials and to be there. The faculty hates to be interrupted, and many talented students have found out the hard way that reference letters from faculty stress how they view you personally as well as how you score on tests. It is also true that many office managers and faculty don't put all the important information in the job manual or in the textbook. Much of this information has to be received in person.

3. True. Patient people are steady, dependable workers who do not rock the boat. Whether it is waiting for the right opportunity or simply being patient enough to keep submitting applications for the perfect job, this quality will pay off. Don't confuse patience with silence however. If you have not heard back by the time you expect, be proactive and make the call or e-mail. Things often get lost or misplaced, and the person who confirms that everything is in order and on time has a huge advantage.

4. True. Not only should deadlines be strictly followed, they should be beaten. While some deadlines may truly be flexible or negotiable, the person involved does not want to have to waste their time talking to you about it. They set the deadline for a reason, and those who finish early will have the best chance to get the job.

5. False. While you may be a charming person, there are bound to be other charming applicants applying for an attractive position. Do the work, be prepared, and then you can relax and show both charm and a mastery of the necessary information.

6. False. How to dress should be part of the research, but there are still companies or college committees who will expect a certain look. If you look unkempt or unprofessional, it will give someone else the advantage. What makes it interesting these days is that some liberal arts colleges or software companies are looking for the socially rebellious, brilliant type. In these situations, showing up in formal dress and looking like a clean-cut businessperson might be a disadvantage. Do the research, and you should find a way to meet the needs of the situation, and be yourself at the same time.

7. True. I don't know how many times I have seen people show up to a conference with their laptop only to find out that it doesn't connect to the presentation projector. Those who are prepared also save their file to a drive that will fit into another computer and prepare a poster or note cards in case the whole system doesn't work. It is surprising how often this happens, and those who can adapt to this trying situation look really good.

8. False. I wish I had a dollar for every time a student tells me they couldn't turn in their paper on time because they finished it right before class, and then the printer didn't work. Sometimes printers run out of toner or stop working at precisely the wrong time. It is critical to attach the document in an e-mail and confirm receipt or print out documents the day before they are needed. It can avoid the loss of a job and keep you out of an embarrassing moment or a zero on an assignment.

9. True. Whether it is a job application, graduate school application, or other important meeting, don't be shy. Call them with a list of questions about what you need to do to be prepared and to get advice. The administrative assistant who answers the phone will usually be very forthright and helpful. If it is possible, set up an appointment to go by in person to get the inside scoop. This type of preparation shows that you really care about doing things the right way, and if you show up well prepared, it shows respect for the time of the people who will meet with you. In a worst-case scenario, maybe they would say that they don't want to give an advantage to anyone, so they couldn't help you. In that case, you

still haven't lost anything and may have planted the seed that you were a go-getter.

10. False. If you know people who have worked at the company, gone to the school, or have another personal connection to a place where you are visiting, by all means bring it up in the conversation. Interviews can be stressful or boring, and this can be a great way to break the ice. Of course, you want to be sure that the person you bring up had a positive reputation with the company and with the person who is interviewing you.

Review

1. Be punctual. There is no going around it, this is critical to a first impression. Arrive ten minutes early for an appointment, and get all application or proposal paperwork one week before the deadline.

2. Look and sound the part. Most places of work expect a certain dress code and have some specific terminology related to their work. The more you match these expectations, the better your chances of getting the position you want.

3. Do your homework. Know who you are meeting, what the position and company are all about, and why you best match the job description.

4. Practice. Practice. Practice. Practice your writing, practice your speaking, practice responses to tough questions.

Self-Evaluation

Rate yourself in each of the categories below from 1 to 10, 1 as the highest rating and 10 the lowest. Be sure to write a comment that explains why you have given yourself this rating.

Attitude   _____   _____

First impressions can make all the difference. What positive traits can you convey in an interview setting? Can you show confidence without being arrogant?

Appearance   _____   _____

Do your hair, clothing, shoes, and personal hygiene make you a good match for the place you want to go? Some places want creativity to show while others are very old-fashioned.

Practice

Set up a practice interview with a friend, relative, career center, or employment agency. Have them rate you from 1 to 10 on the impression you make, and work to improve on any areas that they say might detract from your interview.

Punctuality   _____   _____

The comedian Woody Allen once said 90 percent of life is just showing up. How good are you at this?

Practice

Chart all your events for a week. Include personal obligations and work obligations. Write down the expected times for each of the obligations and the time that you arrived or completed the obligation. Note anything that was done late or forgotten, and check to see if you had it scheduled in a planner or electronic device. Continue to try new methods of writing down and scheduling reminders until you find the right combination for your personal style.

Chapter 2

Motivation: How to Stay Fired Up about Work

Supervisors in every job want to see their employees or students putting sustained energy into their work. This is relatively easy to measure in a classroom environment. For example, if you earn two As and two Cs on exams for a class, you are on track to get a B in the class. Getting the As show that you have the talent, intelligence, or potential to get an A, while the Cs show that you were not able to sustain the top effort on each assignment. Students usually admit that they were lazy with their studying when they received a C or below on an assignment. Some also say that they studied hard, but they didn't understand the material. In both cases, their personal motivation is in question. It takes self-motivation to work hard, and if you don't understand something, it also takes motivation to seek out a boss or a professor during their office hours and ask them how to do something. Students often judge themselves by their top score, while professors use the average. Supervisors in a work environment look at this differently. They see the lowest achievement on an assignment as the amount of effort that they can count on from you and the As or other successes as a bonus that they might get from time to time. The only thing that will impress everyone is to provide a strong and consistent effort, and that takes self-motivation.

It is a common practice for actors to ask directors, "What is my motivation for this scene? "They need to create a level of energy and emotion to match the script. We also hear about the motivation needed to put in all the practice time to become a professional athlete and have seen how the motivation sometimes goes away once the player signs a giant contract. Motivation for work or in college can be difficult to maintain as well.

Unwritten Rules of Chapter 2

You are Evaluated by Your Worst Performance.

Most people consider their best work as representative of what they can do. Motivated people know that supervisors rate your potential by the worst thing on your record. You are much more likely to be eliminated from a job or scholarship from a black mark on your record than you are to win a spot with a good record or good grades. With that in mind, the motivation needs to remain high so that your worst performance is still acceptable.

Show the Passion

When people have equal records, the one who is able to demonstrate their passion and motivation to do the job is the most likely to get it. Success in competition demands a confident and creative approach that highlights how you as an individual will gain from this opportunity and how the job or college will benefit from adding you.

Choose Your Path as Early as Possible

When I ask "What are you motivated to do once you get out of college?" a surprisingly large percentage of students aren't sure. "I don't know. I am just going to finish my degree and then see what happens" is a common response. There are two problems with this.

1. If you are not motivated toward a specific goal for the future, it is easy to do the minimum to get by and not to work hard enough to separate yourself from the competition.
2. If you don't know where you want to end up, you are missing out on opportunities to help you get there.

For example, I had a student a few years ago who decided she wanted to be a meteorologist during her junior year of college. My university doesn't offer a degree in meteorology, and even if it did, the junior year would be late in the process to choose it and still graduate on time.

However, once this student had decided on her path, she was very motivated to get there. She was able to set up an independent study course to earn her first meteorology credits. In addition, I suggested that she research the National Weather Service volunteer program, and she was able to complete a research project with professional meteorologists through this program and present the findings at a national conference in Boston. I am happy to say that this student, despite a late start in the discipline, received a graduate offer. She did need to make up a year of undergraduate work first, but she eventually received an assistantship, finished a master's in meteorology, and is now a professional meteorologist. Her individual motivation to pursue this specific goal really paid off, but first, she had to choose a specific career path and start working on it.

Set Your Goals

Whether it is a job or a college program (and in my mind, they both should be considered professional responsibilities), you must define your motivation. Goals should be set for each of three categories.

> Short term:I need to meet this work quota to get a promotion, or I need this GPA to graduate with honors.
>
> Medium term: I need to be a regional manager within five years, or I need to be finishing my graduate degree.
>
> Long term: My top career goal is _____, and I want to achieve it by _____.

These goals need to be written down as a reminder to keep pushing for them because your current daily work or class schedule may not be enough to keep you motivated on its own.

Develop a Motto

One trick to stay motivated is to develop a personal motto. Mine is "Sean Terry gets things done." While it is surprisingly simple, by taking this motto seriously, I have been able to stay motivated to work harder to complete each task in order to live up to the motto itself. The highest compliment for a motto is when someone else says it independently. Then you know you are on the right track. "Wow, that Sean Terry really gets things done" is exactly what I am working to hear.

I have each of my freshman students develop their own motto. The best advice is to make sure it is easy to remember and it reminds you of a positive quality that you can use to remind you why or how you get things done the best.

Self-Motivation Quiz

	True	False

1. It is most important to prioritize work: that way you can do a great job on the big things and cut corners elsewhere. ⎯⎯⎯ ⎯⎯⎯

2. I get paid for work, so it is more important than the effort I put into college coursework or better job searches ⎯⎯⎯ ⎯⎯⎯

3. Even though I know it is a temporary job, I need to give my best effort and compete with the longer-term employees. ⎯⎯⎯ ⎯⎯⎯

4. I will be moving to a more exciting job in the future, and my coworkers and boss would be impressed to hear about my plans. ⎯⎯⎯ ⎯⎯⎯

5. My boss needs extra help right now, so I should put off work toward my other goals in order to help out. ⎯⎯⎯ ⎯⎯⎯

6. If my friends and family think I am on the wrong career track, I should listen to them and reevaluate my options. ⎯⎯⎯ ⎯⎯⎯

7. I should visit with my boss or my professor even if I am doing well in order to show initiative and get additional advice. ⎯⎯⎯ ⎯⎯⎯

8. I need to outwork everyone on each job or assignment to show that I am the best worker. ⎯⎯⎯ ⎯⎯⎯

9. I should design and follow a motto. ⎯⎯⎯ ⎯⎯⎯

10. Short-term motivation is the most important. ⎯⎯⎯ ⎯⎯⎯

Answers to the Self-Motivation Quiz

1. False. Rather than thinking of cutting corners on some work, it is better not to bite off more than you can chew and to do excellent work at everything. You never know when a current boss at a temporary job might help you (or hurt you) as a reference. The same goes for a college professor. Professors are busy, but they will go out of their way to offer assistantships or reference letters for top students. You never know when they might have a connection to the graduate school or job you ultimately want.

2. False. If you wanted to spend your whole career in your current part-time job, you would be working there full-time. If sacrifices must be made, they should be in the part-time job so that you can more quickly realize the career you really want.

3. True. Full-time workers at restaurants and other jobs are already disposed to dislike the part-timers. Short-term workers are often heading off to exciting places, while the full-times have peaked at this job. Whether it is getting the schedule you want or just having a pleasant work environment, it is important to show motivation and respect to coworkers at your part-time job.

4. False. You should never discuss your grand plans for the future at your current part-time job unless asked. It looks as if you are bragging and can lead to people treating you poorly. Simply show a positive interest in your job and enjoy the fact that a great future is not far away for you.

5. False. I have seen students actually withdraw from college because their part-time boss said they needed more help. What usually happens is that the boss will then put the person on full-time and hope to keep them at a low salary as long as possible. Of course a boss doesn't want to lose a valued, trained employee, but don't let yourself get exploited this way. Once you quit working toward bigger goals, it is easy to settle in and

never reach your potential. Kindly explain that you can't work more hours, and they will usually back down. If they don't back down, there are always other part-time jobs out there.

6. True. Young people are so hell-bent on becoming independent that they often overlook one of their best resources: their friends and family. If these people are unanimous in saying you are on the wrong path, they are probably right. By the way, they are probably right about relationships as well, but that is a topic for a different book.

7. True. It is a great idea to visit with your boss or professor from time to time in an informal way. Ask about an assignment or some aspect of your job and then listen. It shows that you are motivated to do your job well, gives them an opportunity to give you some additional inside information, and makes the boss or professor feel good about you (and themselves).

8. False. I often have top students tell me that they hate group work because other students are lazy and they can't control the final grade as well as if they did all the work themselves. In the real world, most jobs require teams to get the work done. On the job, it is not about beating your fellow workers. The boss is evaluating how you fit in and try to maximize the positive contribution you can make. Be a team player, and things will work out well.

9. True. Some people really live by their personal motto. Others only refer to it occasionally, but a personal motto can be very motivating, like hearing the theme song of your favorite college football team after a touchdown on a game-winning drive.

10. False. Motivation should be spread out between short/medium/long terms. The most important of these will change depending on the situation. Sometimes, the short term needs extra attention. Other times, short-term work becomes boring, and we need to consider the goals of medium and long term to help keep us motivated.

Review

1. Show the passion. Companies want to hire enthusiastic, positive-minded people. Find a way to show that you care about what you are doing and are enthusiastic about the opportunities that their job or class will offer for you.

2. Choose your path as early as possible. You can't get anywhere until you know where you are going. This doesn't mean that you have to take the same path forever, because sometimes we reach dead ends, but it does mean that you should always be moving toward something specific in a decisive way. Always knowing your end destination will keep you motivated along the way.

3. Set your goals. Since the end is usually achieved in a number of steps, it is best to set short-term, medium-term, and long-term goals.

4. Develop a motto. A motto can help keep you motivated and remind you of a positive quality that you can use to get things done.

Self-Evaluation

Rate yourself from 1 to 10 on your organization, and be sure to write why you gave yourself this rating on the line provided.

Self-motivation   _____   _____

Where are you going, and how hard are you working to get there?

Practice

Ask a friend, family, boss, or teacher to rate you for self-motivation. Be sure to ask them to be totally honest if it is a friend or family member. Some people are internally motivated but don't show it. If you are motivated but the people evaluate you lower than you expect in this category, consider ways that you can express your passion and desire to succeed in ways that will be noticed by those around you.

Chapter 3

Get Organized and Stay Organized

Work like a jock? Some of the most successful people I know started out as division 2 athletes. I teach at this level, and over the years, the reason that so many division 2 athletes were successful became clear. They have been forced to organize. They have practice time, games, and road trips that must be fit into their full-time academic schedule. Since most division 2 athletes know they are not going to be professionals at their sport, the scholarships and education are their true reward. Many of them take full advantage of this by practicing good time management and maximizing their potential on the field, in the pool, and in the classroom. Sports teach discipline and hard work, and they reward competitive spirit. In order to succeed in the classroom or on the job, these qualities must be combined with good planning. I have seen athletes stay home on Friday or Saturday night to study while their friends (who were around campus all week but didn't study) go out to party. This combination of discipline and work ethic pays off. The trick is to schedule your whole week and stick to that schedule.

Of course, organization is not always self-evident to athletes. I had one student in class who was a world-class swimmer. This happens occasionally because national team swimmers can't come back to division 1 colleges, but they can attend division 2. This young man had no trouble setting records in the pool and winning a national championship, but he struggled in class. When I asked him about it, he said, "I just can't keep up with all the class assignments, it's too much to remember." I asked him what his next week's swimming schedule would be. "Well, I get up each day at 5 a.m., have breakfast, swim two hours, have two classes, go to lunch, work out with weights, have two more classes, and then swim two more hours. We will be on the road for three days for a swim meet, and I will be swimming in three events over the three days." "Wow," I said. "It seems like you're pretty good at organization. You know every detail of your schedule. Now if you want to graduate, you will need to put the same type of effort into the studying for your classes." Once he was faced with the possibility of not graduating, the student did put in more effort, stopped making excuses, and started passing classes.

Unwritten Rules of Chapter 3:

Writing It Down Doesn't Get It Done

We have to follow up on ideas and assignments and connect with contacts that are written down in the planner. Be sure to move ahead in the planner and put in deadlines for projects and dates to reconnect with contacts so that they don't get lost in previous pages, wasting the effort that it took to gather them in the first place.

Organization Is Not Just for Nerds

All successful people find the right style of planner to keep them on track. Would a nerd schedule a six-week hike in Nepal to a base camp on Mt. Everest? One of my friends did this, and he had to plan two years ahead in order to schedule his work around it. Daily planning keeps us ahead on projects, keeps us from forgetting assignments, and helps us keep up with our friends and colleagues.

Pick the Right Type of Planner

Which type of planning system is right for you? There are different sizes and styles of paper organizers and calendars as well. I like a desktop style that shows one month at a time and has room to write in notes for each day. I also use a computer planner that reminds me about daily appointments. Some of the most sophisticated and easiest-to-use planners can now be updated instantly as applications on your phone. Still, I have colleagues and students who miss out on opportunities (and good grades) by turning things in late. Why?

They procrastinate.

They forget.

They do other things inefficiently and run out of time.

Don't Become a Procrastinator

Why do people procrastinate? People use all types of excuses to justify procrastination. I have heard them all. Some excuses are funny, some are sad, but none of them are acceptable. The classic "the dog ate my homework" has been replaced with "my computer stopped working, and I lost the file." Being busy is not an excuse. Most of us are not nearly as busy as we think we are. Chart out a whole day sometime, in one-half hour increments, and you will see how many unproductive hours there really are in a given day. Television, surfing the Internet, playing on social media sites, or playing video games can all become big time wasters in your life. These are not bad activities, but they must be kept in their place as recreation time so that they don't interrupt work time.

Multitask

One way to get more done in a day is to consider the time period each task takes and allow them to overlap. For example, as I was writing this chapter, I was also doing laundry, canning tomatoes from my garden, and supervising an art project that my son was working on. Clearly this was a weekend day, and a combination of work and fun things need to be done. Each task takes some time, but they can be done simultaneously with the right planning.

Procrastination Is Like Smoking

It is said that many aspects of your personality are genetic, but I believe that procrastination is a learned behavior. It is like smoking: you see other people doing it and you try it. It allows you to avoid doing something you don't want to do for a period of time, and there are elements of it that are attractive and cool. But like smoking, procrastination is a habit that is bad for you. It will hurt your performance and can stunt your career. The only way out of the procrastination habit is to work your way out of it with planning. Keep a planner and update it daily until you get into the good habit of checking it regularly. Now you won't forget appointments, won't be late, and will stay on tasks. Once you get used to it, you will be amazed at how much more can get done and how other good things will begin to happen for you as well.

You Can't Get Too Organized

I have heard from people that they don't want to schedule themselves for each day because it makes life too boring, stifles their creativity, or takes away their ability to be spontaneous. Most of these people have gotten into the habit of procrastinating, and they think daily planning will take up too much time. The most important thing to remember about organization is that it saves you time so you can have more fun time left. Many people don't consider that you need to schedule fun time, free time, vacation time, and other exciting activities in order to keep your life in balance and to give yourself incentive for staying ahead on required work. Scheduled free time can be as spontaneous as you want, and if you need to have a spur-of-the-moment day, you definitely have the right to adjust your planned activities to make up for any missed work later. With regard to creativity, the most creative people in the world, such as musicians, schedule practice time, songwriting time, and recording time. Creativity doesn't just drop from heaven but is partly due to scheduling the time to work on it as well.

Follow Up on Your Opportunities

How many times have you met someone who might be able to help you professionally or seen an article or a phone number that might be useful for you? One of the most prominent items on a business desk of the 1970s was a rolodex, with business cards, phone numbers, and other information alphabetized and at your fingertips. Our tools are even better now. Contacts can be used seamlessly in your phone and computer. Whether it is a new contact number or an idea for a new business, you need to write it down in your planner immediately and set a deadline to follow up on it. People you meet have a limited memory, so it is best to follow up with them in about a week to say hello, remind them that you enjoyed meeting them, and ask questions you may have. Even better would be to follow up with an answer to a question that they had for you. Not all potential contacts work out, but it only takes one to help you find a job or accomplish another goal and make the work to follow up worthwhile.

Organization Quiz

		True	False
1.	Anyone can get organized.	——	——
2.	Being organized is boring.	——	——
3.	Organization stifles creativity.	——	——
4.	You can't be spontaneous if you're organized.	——	——
5.	Organizing leads to more useful free time..	——	——
6.	Following up with new contacts is more important than writing them down in your planner.	——	——
7.	Multitasking beats the one-thing-at-a-time approach.	——	——
8.	Division 2 college athletes are organized.	——	——
9.	Organization can beat talent head-to-head.	——	——
10.	Organization and talent together are unbeatable.	——	——

Answers to the Organization Quiz

1. True. Organization is a learned skill, and while some people are naturally better at it than others, anyone can become organized.

2. False. Organization takes time, but it saves you a lot more time than it takes. This means that it allows you to schedule off time with as many exciting activities as you might like.

3. False. Creative people schedule their work time. Writing is a great example. Good writers schedule plenty of time for outlining, research, writing, and editing. Creative writers need even more time for inspiration, but the mechanics of writing demands daily attention to end up in quality work.

4. False. Being organized does not keep you from being spontaneous. You can block out a day or a week to utilize in a spontaneous fashion, and if that isn't enough, you can make up for an unscheduled spontaneous trip by rescheduling in order to make up for lost time.

5. True. When you schedule your activities, you will be more efficient with your work. This will automatically mean that you have more potential free time.

6. True. New contacts are like buying new fruit at the grocery store. The fruit will go bad within a week. While a contact person may not go bad, they may forget you, which means you lose them. Follow up with contacts, and if at all possible, have something beneficial for them when you call.

7. True. One of the reasons that women are succeeding so well in the modern business world is that they are more comfortable with multitasking than men. Why this is the case is debatable, but regardless of your gender, being more efficient with your time demands that you must be working on several things at a time.

8. True. Take a lesson from division 2 athletes. They have full-time classes, up to six hours of sports per day, and road trips. If they can handle all these and get good grades, it is no wonder that companies and graduate schools come and recruit them. They have demonstrated discipline, organization, and work ethic. Compared to this schedule, most jobs will seem like vacation.

9. True. Ask any college professor, and they will say that they love a hardworking C student better than a brilliant but lazy student who makes an A. These days, most hardworking students will make As. The hardworking, organized student will also make the deadlines, follow up on contacts, and show up for the job interview on time. Which one would you hire? On the job, many talented people get overlooked while steady, hard workers get promoted. It doesn't mean they kiss up; it means they show up and outwork the more talented person.

10. True. Talent combined with organization is an unbeatable combination. I recently had an economics student develop this combination. It began when he wrote a research paper for one of my classes. It was so well done I suggested he work harder on it and submit it to a national conference. The student followed up, did the work and, as an undergraduate, had the paper published and presented at a national conference. This student later applied and received a $35,000 per year fellowship to pursue a PhD in economics at a major university. Yes, that does mean that the college is paying him a good salary to complete graduate school. If you find your talent and are an organized, hardworking person, you will also have this unbeatable combination.

Review

1. Organization is not just for nerds. Work time needs careful planning with our tight schedules. The more efficient you are with work time, the more time is left for other things.

2. Pick a planner style. A planner must be easy to use and easy to understand, or you won't keep it up. Pick one that you like, and stick with it daily.

3. Don't become a procrastinator. There are no good excuses. If you work ahead you can account for real disruptions that come along from time to time.

4. Multitask. Once the daily items you need to accomplish are written down, they can be organized by time frame so that you can simultaneously work on several things.

5. Schedule fun time. Planning is not just for work. It can also allow you to find time for yourself, which is desperately needed as well.

6. Follow up. Once you meet someone or have an idea, don't just let it sit around. Write ahead in your planner to follow up on it. An idea or a new contact person is like a seed. After you plant it, you still need to water and fertilize it, or it will never bloom.

Self-Evaluation

Rate yourself from 1 to 10 on organization, and write a comment that explains your rating in the space provided.

Organization _____ _____

From keeping on track daily to working steadily toward personal and private goals, organization is a big key to success at getting things done.

Practice

Over a weekend, plan out each day of your next week with blocks for work, family or friends, shopping, activities, and other items that fit in your next seven days. Try to stick to the schedule, and compare your productivity and quality of daily life at the end of this week to an unscheduled week.

Chapter 4

Be Proud to Ask for Help

Human communication will always be imperfect. Sometimes people aren't paying attention, so they don't hear directions very well. Other times, the people who are giving instructions aren't clear, leaving you to try to figure out what they mean. There are even situations where you are purposely misled by others. These types of problems in communication can lead to poor grades and lost jobs. The only way to correct the lack of communication is to be willing to ask for help.

Unwritten Rules of Chapter 4:

You Should Ask for Help

Whether it is a big job application or a million-dollar sales proposal, you can ask for help. Application deadlines, procedures, and administrators often change. This can lead to unpublished changes in the rules. Your call to ask about this may even lead to an offer by them to review your entire application and give suggestions on how to improve it. What is the worst thing that can happen? They could say no to the request, at which point you are no worse off than before and at least you know that no other person will get an inside advantage either.

Give Them What They Want

Why ask for help? You are usually working for someone else, and you want to be sure to give them exactly what they want.

My most memorable introduction to the value of asking for help was during the final semester of my master's degree. I had worked hard on my research, read the university guidelines, and thought I had done a very good job with my thesis. Unfortunately, I was wrong, not because I had made research errors, but because I had made a political one. I handed in my thesis to my faculty advisor six weeks before the anticipated graduation. He looked at it briefly and then informed me that it wasn't set up the way he liked, and he didn't think there was any way for me to correct it in time to graduate. Needless to say, I was devastated, attributing all kinds of negative motives for why I was being treated this way. If I didn't graduate, all the time and money I had spent to get here would be wasted! After a day of feeling sorry for myself and asking my friends and family for help, I set up a follow-up meeting with my advisor. In this meeting, I brought an outline of how I would incorporate the recommended changes and agreed to provide the changes as they were written so that they could be approved. This satisfied the professor. I had asked his opinion, and he could see that I was serious about writing the thesis the way he wanted, which after all, is a part of his academic legacy as well. I worked up to eighteen hours per day for the next six weeks and did complete the changes in time, but it was embarrassing and stressful. I haven't repeated this mistake again. It could all have been avoided if I had asked for advice on how to organize my thesis along the way and gotten approval from the boss. Thanks to their own egos, time constraints, or resentment about how they were treated years ago, many supervisors won't take the time to tell you what they expect. They have a sink-or-swim mentality when it comes to your work and will only help if you make the first move and ask for it.

Let Them Help You

Why ask for help? Conditions change. If your application, sales proposal, or grant proposal doesn't match the current format and guidelines, it will be thrown out.

I once lost a $50,000 grant because I didn't know that I should call them and verify the format of my proposal. I was concerned that they might not be willing to answer questions for a competitive grant application. As it turned out, they had changed their format and submission guidelines at the last moment, and the only applications that met the new criteria were those who had called before they sent in their materials and made sure that it was ready to go. I later found out that some panels will even look over your proposal and give you suggestions on how to improve it before you submit it. After that, I realized that not only could I ask questions, but that they *wanted* me to do this. In the four years that followed my initial error, I was able to secure more than $200,000 to support geographic education in Missouri.

Don't Be Too Shy or Too Stubborn

Why ask for help? It saves you time and embarrassment.

Some of my best students have received poor grades on the first research paper in my class. There were two or three elements required in these papers that were new to them, and two things often happen. First, they don't even look at the directions and they write the style of paper that has gotten them good grades in the past. Second, they don't understand the new element that they are expected to add, so they do it incorrectly or don't add it at all. I have the directions clearly written in the syllabus and explained the elements in class, but people don't always pay attention. I have boiled down the various reasons for this type of mistake into two causes: too shy or too stubborn. Shy students are afraid that their question will sound stupid, and they don't want to bother anyone. While there are stupid questions, most supervisors, and professors would rather have people asking some questions rather than sitting there silently. It shows that you care and gives the boss or professor a chance to explain what they want and show their expertise. The stubborn student or employee is a mixed blessing. While independently solving problems is a good trait in some situations, it can waste a lot of time, money, and grades if you are working independently (and stubbornly) in the wrong direction.

Asking for Help Quiz

	True	False
1. You can't ask too many questions.	_____	_____
2. Your peers are usually the best people to ask for help.	_____	_____
3. Your boss or professor wants you to ask for help.	_____	_____
4. Asking for help makes you look weak.	_____	_____
5. Being too independent can get you into trouble.	_____	_____
6. Asking for help is a good political move.	_____	_____
7. It is best to ask for help early in the process.	_____	_____
8. If your boss or professor won't answer your questions, then that is the end of the process.	_____	_____
9. The most successful people ask lots of questions.	_____	_____
10. The Internet is the best place to find answers to questions.	_____	_____

Asking for Help Quiz Answers

1. False. There are limits to anyone's patience. Questions should be limited to the information you really need to know, and you need to be sure not to monopolize a boss or professor's time. There are other people who have questions as well.

2. False. While peers sometimes have good information, they are often wrong as well. In some cases, they might be right but still be wrong. I have often had students say that they asked someone else who had taken a class how to do something, and then they still got a bad grade. In most cases, the other student had taken a different professor, and each class is run a little differently. Only your boss or professor can tell you exactly what they expect and how to achieve it.

3. True. Asking questions shows respect for your work and for your superior. They want you to succeed, not only because it helps you, but because it reflects well on them.

4. False. Weakness is based on performance. Asking the right questions improves your performance, so it makes you look stronger in the end. Don't be stubborn. My college has lots of people to help students: financial aids professionals, counselors, faculty advisors, even career advisors. These services are free (or more correctly, students have already paid for them with their tuition). Sadly, a large percentage of students don't take advantage of these services. Pride, laziness, or a simple lack of understanding the system is to blame, but don't let it happen to you. Use the human network around you, and you will reap the benefits.

5. True. Society may like a rebel, but most supervisors and professors don't. There is room for independent work to make your result stand out, but you must make sure to clarify the expectations of the boss before you begin.

6. True. Asking for help can make you look good. Let's say you are in a meeting, and even though you know the answer to a question, many of your peers do not. By asking this question, you gain credibility with your peers. There are also times when asking the boss or professor a question is a way to stand out in a positive way. If you ask this question in private, you make yourself known as someone who wants to do the job right, and you will be remembered in a positive way.

7. True. Asking questions about a project right before it is due is disrespectful to a professor and adds stress to a boss at work. It is best to work ahead so you can ask the right questions very early in the process.

8. False. Maybe your boss is too busy to answer your question. Maybe they don't like you for some reason. In academics, it is perfectly acceptable in this case to go up to a department chair level and ask your question there. This must be an important question, however, as word of this may be considered going behind the back of your boss. In the case that the boss is doing something wrong in the first place, their supervisor can only find this out if questions are asked by employees, so they will want to know.

9. True. Whether it is Bill Gates or the president of the United States, successful people ask lots of big questions, and they surround themselves with people who are good at finding answers. One of the best ways to distinguish yourself in a class or on the job is to independently research a question that comes up and bring that answer back. This process shows research skill and personal initiative. The only potential problem is if you do it so much that people call you a know-it-all. In real life, I think the US president could really use a know-it-all if they were correct on all their points of research.

10. False. While it is possible to find answers to lots of questions online, it is equally likely that you will get incorrect or misleading

information. Wikipedia is a great example of this. When this came out, the answers on Wikipedia were not researched and were often wrong. They did not meet an academic standard for research, but students utilized this source exclusively in some cases. Now that links to primary sources of information have been added to Wikipedia, it is now a tool to help find some answers quickly. Another thing that is missed when independently finding things online is the personal assistance of a boss, professor, or librarian, who could help you not only find the answer to this question but also help you develop the valuable skills of research so that you can more easily find the answer to the next question as well.

Review

1. Give them what they want. They only way to know exactly what someone wants is to ask them.

2. Let them help you. Sometimes directions are not clear on applications, grant proposals, or work assignments. Sometimes the directions are clear, but the conditions have changed in the last year without all the new guidelines being printed. Asking how to do it right will save you time and will save them the time of reading a bad application.

4. Don't be too shy. You will not be yelled at for asking a question in a respectful way 99.9 percent of the time. Speak up. There are probably several other people who are wondering the same thing, but they are too shy to ask as well.

5. Don't be too stubborn. The time to work independently is after you fully understand the assignment and all aspects related to it. Remember, getting involved in the discussion of a work assignment is important for political reasons as well as for academic ones.

Self-Evaluation

Rate yourself from 1 to 10 on how well you ask for help. Write a comment that explains your rating in the space provided.

Asking for help　　　_____　_____

You don't want to be a pest, but asking questions shows respect to a professor or boss and allows you to efficiently use your time to complete projects the right way.

Practice

During a work week, write down questions as they come to mind. Consider the urgency of each question, and write down the response that you received when you asked the question.

Subjects below are examples of times when you should ask the question.

1. There is money involved.
2. You don't know a rule for a class or business procedure.
3. Giving the wrong answer could hurt your chances at a job or in a class.
4. Assuming the worst without checking could hurt someone else's feelings.
5. Your supervisor is the expert and would expect you to ask out of respect.
6. There are multiple possible answers, and the only way to get the one that fits this situation is to ask someone with experience.
7. Something was told to you already, but you forgot it or lost the notes. In this case, it would be more beneficial to ask a peer for help than to ask a supervisor to repeat information they have already provided.

Chapter 5

Learn to Be Part of a Group

Pull your weight, and work will be in harmony.

When I was a teenager, my family had a music show in Branson, Missouri. We played there in the summer and traveled and played music around the country at other times of the year. We even had a bus like the *Partridge Family* (a TV show about a music family from the 1970s). My mother was the obvious leader of the show. She was the primary singer, played the piano, selected the songs, and arranged our music. She even sewed our outfits. My father played guitar, banjo, or bass guitar and sang. I played the drums and sang, and my two sisters were the support singers up front. While I didn't realize it at the time, the years I spent in a family music show taught me some valuable lessons about group-working skills. The first lesson is that everyone has to pull their weight. As the drummer, I needed to be the anchor of each song. It wouldn't matter how perfectly my mother sang or played the piano; if the drummer was off beat, the song would sound terrible. There is no place to hide on a stage, so you better know your part. In addition to performing your own role, everyone has to be on the same page with each other. This can only come with hard work done together. The result from not being a good group worker in music is obvious: silence or even boos. This motivates musicians to work harder or to find another line of work. The rewards and failures of group work in college or on the job are much harder to quantify. There is usually a project at stake and a grade or contract to earn, but many people coast through these assignments, assuming someone else will take up the slack. Don't fall into this trap. Think of your team as a music group and your individual part as a critical beat or harmony that is needed to hold it all together.

Unwritten Rules of Chapter 5:

Build Trust Early, and It Will Feel Great to Be a Part of a Group

The biggest complaint I hear about group work is that people prefer to work alone. They are comfortable with their own abilities and don't trust the work ethic or the intelligence of others. How do you get past this? Musicians build trust through practice. In a work or school environment, the best practice is to set a very specific and quick deadline for each member of a work group and meet together to go over the results. Once everyone has shown they can pull their weight, the obvious benefits of sharing ideas, dividing workload, and utilizing individual talents can make the rest of the work much more fun and productive than solitary work.

Group Work Can Be Fun

Most college students claim that they don't like group work. The leaders complain that other students are not carrying their weight, and the following students claim that they were never given a chance to contribute. So why do we faculty assign it? The primary reason we assign group work is to give students practice in the valuable skill of working with others. Whether you are a towel person at a car wash or the CEO of a global company, you will work with a group at work. It is much better to learn the lessons of working with others in class rather than to learn these lessons when your paycheck and professional reputation are on the line. In order to get paid, everyone will need to work with groups. The more effective you are at communicating with others and performing your role within a group, the more quickly you will succeed in life.

Be the Leader that Works the Smartest

Many leaders make the mistake of thinking that they are the best persons at everything in their group. This assumption leads to them putting in more hours than everyone else and micromanaging the work of others.

This doesn't usually lead to better results. The best group leaders recognize the skills of others and trust them to do their job. Delegation is the key. Great managers realize that giving people the tools they need and properly motivating them are their most important roles. Then each person is doing something fulfilling, taking responsibility, contributing their talent, and evolving professionally. A leader must pull their weight, but they don't have to put in any more hours than the people working with them.

Don't Assume Your Leader Is an Idiot

Many new employees who fancy themselves future leaders are asked to assume a following role in order to learn the ropes. They often question the style or motives of their leader as out-of-date, uninformed, or just plain stupid. There are definitely some idiots out there, but most of the time, there are good reasons to explain why people do things in a certain way. The first thing to do in this case is to remain humble and ask for clarification. The answer will usually be based on business or political experience and is probably something that the new worker has never faced or considered before. It is important to learn these reasons as you develop your own leadership skills. If the answer is given to you but it still doesn't make sense and this opinion is unanimous among all the followers in the group, then it is time for the group to meet together and bring up the issues at hand in a respectful way. If there is still a problem after this meeting, then it is time to inform the next person up the chain of command that there is a communication problem and ask for their advice.

Be a Good Follower

The world needs a lot more followers than leaders, so most people do spend the majority of their lives as followers. This is a choice for people who don't want the spotlight. There are many assistant coaches in college football who have passed on the opportunity to be head coaches because they like their limited role and the money they make is good enough for them. The same is true on other businesses. Some people like middle management. They don't have big pressure, make enough money for their family, and usually have more flexibility for their private life.

Followers are just as valuable as leaders. While their primary role may be to do their own part of a project, they also need to support others and to bring up questions that help keep everyone on the same track. Most new positions in graduate school and the workplace will be following positions. Followers are expected at a minimum to do these things:

1. Be on time.
2. Show up for meetings.
3. Stay caught up on all the research to understand the project.
4. Offer to do more if their part goes more quickly or easily than other people in the group.
5. Show an understanding of the chain of command for the project, and be willing to serve as a leader if the work situation demands it.

Just Get Along

Group work is usually a temporary assignment. It is ideal if each person in a group works extremely hard and everyone likes each other, but it is not usually the case. The end product is the most important thing, not whether everyone becomes friends or that everyone has an identical workload. The leader has to be especially aware to help avoid personal conflicts and to fairly distribute the work. Many people who adopt the role of leader try too hard to make the rest of the team happy. Being too accessible or too friendly can encourage individuals or the whole team to take advantage of the leader. The leader should be friendly but firm and consistent with the group about goals, deadlines, and other details. Lazy or sloppy work should be addressed in person immediately. Personality conflicts should also be brought in the open right away and resolved. If the work does not improve after a personal mention, then it is time to consult a supervisor and see if they can use leverage to get everyone motivated to complete the project as a group.

Group work is not just a necessary evil. Shared resources are greater than the knowledge or ability of any one person. That is the reason we are put in groups in the first place. If you can distinguish yourself as good at working with groups, you will be well on the way to a successful life.

Group Work Quiz

		True	False
1.	You should do the work for lazy team members to stay on schedule to complete group tasks.	___	___
2.	Good leaders outwork everyone else.	___	___
3.	The boss should be kept in the loop on group work.	___	___
4.	Group followers should be silent and do their tasks.	___	___
5.	It is OK to ignore the leader if the person is an idiot.	___	___
6.	You need to like people to work well with them.	___	___
7.	When there is a problem, you should address it in person first and then go to a supervisor if the problem is not resolved.	___	___
8.	The leader will get more credit than the rest of the group.	___	___
9.	It is important to know about all aspects of a project.	___	___
10.	Group work should be a true democracy.	___	___

Group Work Quiz Answers

1. False. If you are working ahead and someone is not doing the work, they should be urged to stay on task. If they don't respond, it is up to the supervisor to either motivate them or remove them from the project. Doing the work for the person is an unfair addition to your work and sets a bad example for the lazy employee.

2. False. Good leaders work the same amount, and part of their workload is to properly delegate work and motivate the group.

3. True. Even if they choose not to read each e-mail, the boss likes to know what is going on and whether things are on track. This gives them the opportunity to step in if things are going in the wrong direction.

4. False. Group followers have an obligation to speak up if they have a good idea, a solid criticism, or a creative thought.

5. False. There are many reasons for people's actions, but they are usually not an idiot. They may not respect you or may have knowledge or experience that you lack. In any case, it is important to pay attention and ask questions to determine why things are being done in a certain way and to contribute ideas that may improve the progress of a group project.

6. False. While it is nice to like people in your work group, it can sometimes be a disadvantage. Especially if a couple of people are good friends and the rest get left out of the inside information between them. The best groups see their task as a professional goal and treat each team member respectfully and equally.

7. True. A supervisor will not have the time to address each petty issue that comes up. On the other hand, they do want to intervene before a work or personality conflict puts a project behind schedule. When it is appropriate, the supervisor does wield the appropriate leverage to get the problem resolved.

8. True. The rewards for successful leadership are the positive credit, compliments, good grades, or bonus pay that you receive. There is risk to leadership, and that risk is rewarded when things go well. Of course the risk also means the leader gets more credit if things go wrong as well, which is why some people are comfortable to be followers for life.

9. True. Group work demands cooperation and understanding of all aspects. This way, good ideas can be shared and duplication of work can be minimized.

10. False. While the idea of democracy is a good one, most projects don't work that way. There is usually a group leader and then a boss over that level. Making big decisions and staying on track require this leadership. Group input is valuable, but true democracy in meetings and projects can be very inefficient of time and resources.

Review

1. Group work can be fun. If assignments are equal and clear, the shared creative energy of a group can make this type of work more fun and productive than independent work.

2. Be the leader who works the smartest. Volunteering for leadership shows initiative, adds control, and can lead to personal advancement. If you utilize those around you properly, leadership doesn't require you to work any more hours than other team members. A good leader will trust and delegate. Shared work must be just that, and a dominating leader stifles the ability and fun of a group.

3. Don't assume your leader is an idiot. Leaders usually have a reason for their style and their requests for you. Be sure to ask for that reason before thinking negatively about the person or the assignment.

4. Be a good follower. A good follower does their share. In addition to doing their share of the work, an even better follower will offer to do more if they work ahead of schedule and will keep up with everything that is going on.

5. Just get along. You don't have to like everyone in a group. The only requirement is to get the work done. Don't worry about personal differences unless they hurt the project.

Self-Evaluation

Rate yourself from 1 to 10 on your skills as a group worker. Add comments to explain your rating in the space provided.

Group-working skills _____ _____

How well do you lead, follow, trust, and delegate in a group working environment? It is the only way to have productive long-term work relationships.

Practice

Use the following strategy with your next group-work assignment.

1. The group must meet and agree together on all work assignments and have a specific schedule for meetings and deadlines that is written down. Before assigning anything, ask each member to write down what skills they feel that they can contribute to the project and have the group agree to match the skills to the work assignments.
2. If someone doesn't meet a deadline or does poor work, the group must let them know immediately in person if possible. If it is by e-mail, than the supervisor should be copied on the communication so that everyone is aware of the situation.
3. If someone doesn't shape up right away when they are informed about their lack of performance, it is time to tell the supervisor. A personal meeting with the boss or professor will contain the leverage to solve this problem once and for all. Either the person will agree to pull their weight or they will be taken off the group project.

Chapter 6

Find Good Team Chemistry

There is a very popular book that says everything you need to know to succeed is taught in kindergarten. I am not so sure that is true, but I can definitely say that I have witnessed the power of team chemistry at that age. I coached soccer for my son's team in kindergarten and first grade, and there is nothing quite as funny or rewarding as seeing those kids play soccer. At practice the first day, some children cry and won't even leave their parent's protective side to take the field. I had one young man who even hid under a blanket and wouldn't come out. He said he liked it under there. Even when they do get on the field, the children move around in a blob, following the ball, and kicking each other and falling down more than working as a team. When they fall, shoes and glasses fly everywhere, and there is a five-minute delay to check for boo-boos. With practice, coaching, and encouragement, this gets better as the weeks go on. The kids find friends and develop trust in the coach. They start to learn to pass the ball and defend with more confidence. They even learn that falling down doesn't usually hurt and can often be avoided. My son didn't score a goal on his own in the first year, but he still vividly recalls the moment when he saw a teammate and made a perfect setup pass that allowed us to score a goal. It was the first team goal, and the chemistry (and our win/loss record) kept getting better after that.

Unwritten Rules of Chapter 6:

Team Chemistry Is Enhanced by Diversity

These days, businesses and colleges are stressing the importance of attracting and retaining diversity. Diversity can be defined in many ways. On a sports team, individual differences in skill are more significant than racial background, ethnicity, or nationality. In a work environment, the wider range of life experience and academic skills, the more likely it is that people will be able to feed each other's skills and experience and generate new ideas from them. I have experimented with this in the classroom. I chose some teams with all students in the same major while choosing other teams with widely different backgrounds and majors. In almost all occasions, the more diverse team came up with a more creative, thoughtful, successful project than the more homogeneous team. If you think of this like a chemistry set, the more different ingredients you have, the more possibilities you can create from combining them.

Know Your Role on the Team

Group dynamics must begin with the assignment of roles. In sports, this is pretty easy. The coach matches up the size, speed, and skill of players to the positions where their skills will be most beneficial. Players have practice to prove themselves, and the team is reevaluated after each game. In most jobs, assigning and evaluating teamwork is much more challenging. Usually, there is a hierarchy determined by tenure (the length of time someone has worked there) or by talent. The boss has to choose teams for individual projects or may look at the whole company as one team. In either case, those who succeed and advance will have to prove themselves trustworthy and talented enough to keep their position.

Football is the most popular professional sport in America. Let's compare work skills to football positions to demonstrate how a boss might look at a corporate team.

Coach: The person who knows the answers, has the plan, and teaches the players how to maximize their potential.

Coach: Boss, professor, or mentor. The person who can provide the answers, mentor students and employees, and help design the best plan for their success.

Speed: The wide receiver or running back. The ability to break away and score quickly for the team.

Speed: The fast, efficient worker. The ability to quickly reply to calls and e-mails or to quickly research and write a proposal. Just as in sports, speed is a requirement for modern work.

Offense: The offensive lineman. The ability to protect and support the offense so they can move down the field and score points.

Offense: Technical support specialist. These workers are critical to keep technology running and up-to-date. They can also support the team by providing an advantage with new and innovated technical solutions to problems. This will help the company "score" winning proposals.

Defense: The defensive line. These players stop the advance and the attack of the opponent to keep them from scoring.

Defense: The researcher and/or legal team. The ability to provide research support to a team is a critically useful position. Research can be used to stay ahead of the competition or to "defend" a company from claims that the opponent may be trying to use to gain an advantage.

Quarterback: The team leader. The quarterback needs to demonstrate knowledge, earn trust, and be able to respond under pressure to help the team win.

Quarterback: The team leader. This individual also needs to be good at critical thinking, demonstrating knowledge, earning trust, and being able to respond under pressure to help a business or academic team win.

Even if your boss or professor doesn't like sports, they still are looking for team members who can demonstrate the skills listed above. Those who do will be rewarded.

Show Team Leadership

Team leaders are easy to pick out. The best leaders are good at evaluating the talent of everyone on their team and giving each person a relevant part of the work that matches their skills. This will keep the individual interest level up and keep everyone happy as the project evolves. Good leaders are extremely organized and call just enough meetings to keep everyone informed and motivated. As a reward for their work, leaders generally get most of the credit, promotions or bonuses, and control of the project. They also get new experiences and are allowed to work with the boss more closely. The benefits can be financial, personal, and political, so don't be afraid to volunteer to lead something.

Have a Mentor

Young people often don't want a mentor. They are tired of being told what to do by parents and teachers and ready to test their own skills against the world. What they usually find out is that they still have a lot to learn. Not only that, but their independent, stubborn streak hurts team chemistry. The only way to learn the specifics of a new job, graduate school, or other challenge is to find someone who has been there to help you navigate these new waters. Athletes have a coach, and now some businesses are offering "life coaches." I recommend that you look for someone in your chosen field who is where you want to be in the future and make an appointment. A mentor can give good advice and good references and can help you avoid the pitfalls of a new challenge.

Be a Mentor

The best way a team builds chemistry is to have the more experienced players help the new players learn the system. In addition to finding a great role model to help you, it is also possible to get benefits from helping your own peers or those who are following your path but still a year or more behind. Being a mentor will expand your network, giving you future friends and personal satisfaction. My greatest academic satisfaction comes when one of my students successfully finishes graduate school or lands their dream job. Over the years, as these former students have stayed in touch, they have started to become leaders in their fields and spread out all over the world. I have since received great ideas for research, up-to-date advice on careers for students, and national and international connections for travel. These benefits have more than paid off for the extra time I spent to help personally mentor these individuals.

Another surprising benefit of being a mentor is that it makes you better at what you do. When I was a teaching assistant, I had to review all the key concepts of my field so that I could teach them to others. By mentoring other students, I actually reinforced and built on the depth of my own knowledge of the subject.

Show Empathy

One of the best methods to build team chemistry and trust is to show empathy toward them. Everyone has a bad day, a clumsy day, or an inappropriate comment from time to time. We all expect other people to forgive when this happens to us but often hold others to a higher standard when they make a mistake. Take the time to ask how people are doing when they are having a problem and listen to the answer. Knowing that you understand and care about them will cause them to give you some slack when it is your turn to have a bad day.

Seek Out Diversity

A life full of diverse food, music, culture, and people is an interesting life. A life that is too homogenous is likely to be a boring life. In addition to the obvious benefits of new experience, diversity also inevitably leads to new ideas and new opportunities. I once worked for Red Lobster restaurant, breading shrimp as a college job. A woman from Cameroon, Africa, Agnes, was doing the same. We started talking during the long hours, and I ended up learning more about African geography from those conversations than I ever learned in a geography class. Would anyone suggest that people who want to learn about African geography should get a job breading seafood? Probably not, but it shows that if you don't engage new people in conversation, you never know what knowledge, connections, or ideas you may gain.

Team Chemistry Quiz

		True	False
1.	A more homogenous team is more effective.	——	——
2.	After college, you still need a mentor.	——	——
3.	Being a mentor is just an unpaid job.	——	——
4.	Talent is more important than team chemistry.	——	——
5.	A coach/mentor has to be tough to be good.	——	——
6.	Defense is more important than offense.	——	——
7.	Clubhouse leaders are as important as field leaders.	——	——
8.	Shrimp breading is the best way to learn about Africa.	——	——
9.	Regular jobs have tryouts for new positions.	——	——
10.	The most experienced person usually gets the best job.	——	——

Answers to the Team Chemistry Quiz

1. False. In my experience, the more diverse team brings more ideas, creativity, and better-researched solutions to the average project than a homogenous team.

2. True. High school and college offer advisors and mentors, but the real world is even more difficult to navigate. It takes effort to find and maintain them, but good professional mentors are extremely important to cultivate.

3. False. Being a mentor can lead to valuable experiences and a vibrant, growing personal network. In the long run, these experiences can lead to personal friendships, professional opportunities, and travel possibilities.

4. False. If this were true, the New York Yankees would win the World Series in baseball every year. Talent will always be important, but chemistry is equally or more important.

5. False. There are many different styles of reaching people. Some people need strong leadership, while others shrink away from aggressive methods. For them, support and encouragement are more motivating than tough talk.

6. False. Defense and offense are equal. All parts of the team must function well on a team or in a business in order to achieve success.

7. True. Clubhouse leaders are as important as field leaders. Field leaders may have more sheer talent, but showing leadership, humor, empathy, or intelligence can add just as significantly to team goals as the talent of one person.

8. False. In my case, this may have been true, but that was a once-in-a-lifetime connection. This example does show, however, that knowledge can come from a variety of sources, if you keep your mind and your ears open for it.

9. True. Regular jobs may not talk about it, but they are always evaluating the progress of employees. In essence, you are always trying out for a higher position in this job or for your next job.

10. False. This used to be the rule, but it has changed. We see this especially with professional sports, where the youngest general manager in baseball led the Boston Red Sox to two World Series victories. In today's workplace, skills and competency in new methods and new technologies is often the top priority in new hires and promotions, not age.

Review

1. Know your role on the team. Many big mistakes happen because people don't know their job description or haven't had their role written down or explained for them. Knowing these expectations and limits can allow you to avoid serious conflicts.

2. Show team leadership. People will want to be your teammates if you show initiative and respect to them.

3. Have a mentor. Good mentors are hard to find, but if you are actively looking for them and purposely keeping in touch, they can help make important opportunities open up for you.

4. Be a mentor. Being a mentor is even more fun than having a mentor and has many of the same rewards.

5. Show empathy. Be there for teammates when they are having a bad day, and they will return the favor.

6. Seek out diversity. A complex world needs multiple perspectives: embrace them.

Self-Evaluation

Rate yourself on team chemistry from 1 to 10. Use the space provided to add comments that explain your rating.

Team chemistry   _____   _____

Rate yourself on the ability to support good team chemistry at work or school.

Practice

Next time you are upset with someone you work with or go to school with, consider whether this is a pattern of behavior or may just be a sign that they are having a problem in some other part of their life that is affecting their behavior today. If it is not a pattern and you need to work with the person, ask them how they are doing. This simple question may lead them to giving a very logical reason for their current problem and building team chemistry with you.

Chapter 7

Build a Network that Works for You

The geography program at Drury University was not advertising a position when my wife and I moved to Springfield, Missouri. My wife had transferred to Springfield so that I could be closer to my family, and my career had to take a backseat for my responsibility to my parents. When I was looking for a job, my sister's best friend happened to be the secretary of the history, political science, and geography department at Drury. When I submitted my CV to the department, she was able to add a valuable character reference that helped get an interview. The department chair even helped me understand how my skills could be used to help teach some classes that they had been having a hard time staffing. That fall, I began teaching part-time for the university. When a full-time position was advertised two years later, I had been able to build a positive teaching reputation for that exact job description, and I landed the job.

Unwritten Rules of Chapter 7:

A Great Network Is Hard Work to Build and Maintain

Professors won't usually come to you and offer to write glowing reference letters. Your former boss will not stay in touch with you and continue to forward you new job offers. It is up to you to make the effort to find your mentors, to let them know you want to use them as references, and to keep them up-to-date with your progress. It is also up to you to thank references in person or with a handwritten, personalized thank-you note. Finally, it is up to you to provide all the information needed to let them write you a great reference letter and to get it in on time. In my opinion, a great reference letter from a person who has a personal connection or reputation with the place you are applying is the single most valuable commodity you can have to win the right job or the graduate fellowship of your dreams.

Know When You Can't Win

While personal connections can definitely help you, they can sometimes hurt as well. When I had first completed my PhD, I submitted my application and interviewed for several faculty positions. In one case, I was interviewed and then offered the job by the search committee, but my contract was denied by the president of the university. In this case, the president was retiring and had chosen to appoint his personal assistant to the job. This was a seriously frustrating case, which violated hiring ethics, and I threatened to go to court to get my contract. When I contacted a lawyer, he informed me that the outgoing president was the former governor of the state, and if the case did go to court, it would be in front of a judge that he had appointed. Clearly, it was time to cut my losses and move on. Whether it is a current employee's spouse, friend, or other connection, there are times when your qualifications will not matter. The only thing to do in this case is to limit your investment of time and effort once it becomes clear that you are not the primary candidate. In most cases, this is probably not the ideal job for you anyway. Politely thank them for the opportunity, and realize that there are always benefits to practicing the interview process and that it is a compliment to be selected even if you are not ultimately chosen.

Write Down and Keep Up with Your Contact List

Who do you know who could help you? Take the time at each of the levels below to list the names and contact information of each person who might be able to help you, and also list in what capacity they might be of assistance. Update their contact information annually, and contact them personally once a year with an update of your achievements and contact information.

Utilize Grandparents and Parents

Younger people often don't take advantage of the connections and life experience that their grandparents and parents have amassed in their lifetime. Visit with them about it. It is very likely that they know several people who would know of a job, have a connection to a college, or could write a reference letter that would give you an advantage. Parents also can check and see if their work or other social connections offer college scholarships or paid internships. Many businesses and some social groups such as Shriners offer scholarships, but some of this money goes unclaimed because people don't ask about it and follow up with the application.

Use Old-Fashioned Social Networking

The primary reason that most people go to church is religious, but there can be tremendous political advantages as well. Some businesses even recommend certain churches to employees who move in from out of town as "the right place to meet the right people" in their community. Church leaders are usually very well connected and well respected in their communities. They can provide formal or informal reference to help people find the right job. Nonprofit agencies can also serve this role. The leaders of charity organizations need to be politically active to allow their businesses to survive, so they know a lot of important people, as well as a diverse group. In addition to making these contacts, you never know who else you might run into when volunteering. Imagine that you are an architecture student and you volunteer to help build a house for Habitat for Humanity. Not only is this a rewarding experience but it puts you in contact with local architects who might hire you in the future. This is a win-win situation that many people never consider.

Initiate Boss Networking

Every boss is a potential future reference. This is especially true of college professors. They know how former students have succeeded. They also know people in the community and people in their research specialty that could help a student get a job or a graduate assistantship. Many students don't know how to take advantage of this resource.

Whether it is a boss at work or a professor, this must be done in a private conversation. Explain your goals and ask the person if they would be willing to serve as a reference. If you have several potential references, do the research to find out which one of them might have a personal connection with the position that you want. They may know someone, be a graduate of the same university, or have met someone at a conference that might help you get the job. Many will go this far, but the next part is what separates those people who get a reference letter from those who get a glowing, fantastic, personally tailored reference letter. The ones who get the great letter usually get the job or the graduate school opportunity that can change their life for the better.

Network Contact Reference Sheet

Name _____

Business _____

Date First Met _____

Most Recent Contact Date _____

Phone Number _____

Fax Number _____

E-mail Address _____

Website Address or Other Contact Information _____

Experience or Connections That This Reference Can Provide

_____

_____

_____

Friends or Other Colleagues of This Contact That Can Be Utilized As Well

_____

_____

_____

Times and Dates That This Contact Has Been Used for Job Reference or Reference Letter

_____

_____

_____

_____

Request a Reference the Right Way

When you request for a reference letter, there are some rules to follow. First, you need to write a cover letter that politely asks for the reference and explains why you are applying for this position. It should briefly explain why you feel this person's reference letter will help you get the position. The cover letter should never be longer than one page. Then you need to provide the person whom you want to write the letter with the following:

1. Title of the position for which you are applying
2. Name and title of the person or committee to whom the letter is to be addressed
3. Full and exact address for the letter and a completed, addressed, and stamped envelope
4. Deadline by which the letter needs to be sent, giving the person all possible notice
5. A current résumé that includes all experience that you have that the person can utilize to help write a stronger letter

If you haven't seen the reference letter writer in a while, remind them of the work that you did for them and why this was a valuable experience for you.

E-mail, call, or even better, go by in person to make sure they have received the request.

Upon confirmation of the submission of the letter, write a thank-you note.

Network with Your Peers

Despite the fact that they have a similar life experience with yours, peers can be extremely valuable networking partners. Perhaps the biggest advantage is that you have equal leverage as an opportunity to help them and that peer connections can be there for a lifetime. Whether it is a sorority, fraternity, close friends from high school, or people you have met on the job, these people can be utilized to help find answers and opportunities. The college Greek system is a great example. Fraternities and sororities have national networks of people who could offer you a job. The only requirement is to distinguish yourself in some way, whether it is through service, in a leadership role, or by attending conferences. These activities will provide you a launching pad for meeting the people who can help you reach your highest goals. A recent president of Drury University was also a graduate of Drury. During his college years, he had a great time, finished his degree, and made strong friendship connections that have lasted a lifetime. The people who were peers and students in college went on, in some cases, to be captains of businesses, members of boards of trustees, and distinguished doctors and lawyers. It is easy to see that these people would be helpful to anyone later in life, and all you need to do is to stay in touch with them to reap the benefits of such connections. It has often been said that the shared knowledge of any group of students exceeds the knowledge of any professor. I am not sure if this is true, but I have seen how successful and efficient job searching can be when students share information with each other.

Network with the Administrative Assistant

Who is the one person who knows everything in an office? I think the best advice my father ever gave me regarding business was to treat administrative assistants with respect. They know what is going on below you, at your level, and above you. They can tell you who writes good reference letters or steer you away from people who may harm your chances of getting a job. If you are friendly and helpful with them, good things seem to happen. This is also true of professionals who work in human resources, alumni associations, or career centers. They are busy people who take a lot of criticism. The last thing they need is a stressed-out person demanding services from them. On the other hand, if you are have a positive attitude and you stay in touch with these people in the appropriate way, they will seek you out when they hear of an opportunity that matches your needs.

Maintain and Grow Your Network

The old rolodex of cards with written names is no longer on our desks. Now we have electronic options to keep contact information and to keep in touch. Electronic social networks can help keep contact information up-to-date, meet deadlines, and communicate with people to stay fresh in their minds. It is not important which software option you choose, but it is important to take the initiative when it comes to communication. Each important contact should be contacted annually with an update of how you are doing, what you are doing, and a request to keep their contact information up-to-date. This is important beyond records. Keeping your name in the minds of people allows them to keep you in mind when opportunity knocks. It takes effort to build up a good network, but many networks are lost over time because they are not maintained. There are definitely people who will fade away in importance and can be deleted over time. Hopefully, for each person that is eventually deleted from the list of contacts, one or two new people will be added.

Networking Quiz

		True	False
1.	Who you know is more important than what you know when it comes to getting a job.	___	___
2.	A grandparent might help you get a job.	___	___
3.	Getting a reference letter is the ultimate goal.	___	___
4.	Always use your three favorite references for letters.	___	___
5.	All your network should be your electronic friends.	___	___
6.	People will remember you and let you know if opportunities that fit your skills and experience appear.	___	___
7.	Fraternity connections can win you a job.	___	___
8.	Volunteering is a win-win opportunity.	___	___
9.	Quantity is more important than quality when it comes to maintaining networking contacts.	___	___
10.	The most important person who can help or hurt you in the office is the administrative assistant.	___	___

Answers to the Networking Quiz

1. False. Who you know might get you an interview, but in the long run, you still need to have strong references and demonstrate your ability to do the job. It is too easy for some people to fall into the trap of feeling that every job is decided by politics and to become negative about it. You may get an advantage or disadvantage based on who you know, but if you are qualified and prepared, your opportunities will come.

2. True. Many potential sources of knowledge and assistance go untapped. I am continually amazed at how friends, relatives, cousins, church members, parents, coworkers, and even more distant connections can provide help or information that can help you get the position you want.

3. False. The ultimate goal is to have your application be selected above all the rest. They will all have reference letters. Your reference letters need to be noticeably better, more direct, and personal in order to accomplish this goal.

4. False. The best reference is usually the person who has the most solid personal connection to the job or the place that you are applying. This requires that you make a strong-enough connection with this reference to get the right letter.

5. False. It is very likely that you have some personal information or friends who write unprofessional things on your other friends' electronic sites. It is best to keep professional contacts on a professional social networking site or to simply contact them via e-mail.

6. False. No matter how impressive you are, managers and professors meet new people constantly. The only way to have them think of you and remember you is if you contact them at least once per year with an update.

7. True. Fraternity peers, administrators, or potential employers who were members of your Greek organization could all work to your advantage if you have made a positive contribution to this organization.

8. True. Volunteering feels good, and it is a great networking opportunity. Choosing charities that match your professional goals makes that charity work more enjoyable while also exposing you to people who could help you achieve your professional goals.

9. False. Having a broad and diverse list of networking contacts is helpful, but there are limits to how many people can be part of the inner circle of people who will go out of their way to help you. Besides this, if the list gets too big, it will be impossible to maintain personal updates with each of them. In the end, it is probably better to have ten great people in your network than to have fifty people on the list but with no personal connection with any of them.

10. True. Don't make the mistake of ignoring or mistreating the administrative assistant. This person knows much more than you do about how things really operate, and all paperwork passes along this desk. For getting positive things done or avoiding potential problems, the administrative assistant is your best possible ally.

Review

1. Know when you can't win. Sometimes another person's personal network is better set up to get a particular job than yours. Even if you are better qualified, there are times you can't win. When this happens, politely move on.

2. Write down and keep up with your contact list. Update contact information annually and send updates to your contacts about your progress.

3. Utilize grandparents and parents. These people are always on your side and know a lot of other people who may be able to help you.

4. Use old-fashioned social networking. Joining social clubs, attending church, and other group activities can lead to great new references.

5. Initiate boss networking. Supervisors are busy, but they will usually help you if you ask politely and especially if you have done a good job for them.

6. Request a reference the right way. Always give plenty of lead time, all pertinent information about your qualifications, and all information about the application committee, job title, address, etc., to the person asked to write a reference letter.

7. Network with your peers. They are in the same boat and the same generation with you. If you all share knowledge, you will all succeed together.

8. Network with the administrative assistant. It is always good to be in good standing with the people who know everything that is happening.

9. Maintain and grow your network. A network is like a garden. It needs attention, but you can reap the fruits of that labor in the long run.

Self-Evaluation

Rate yourself from 1 to 10 on networking. Write comments in the space provided to explain your rating.

Networking contacts _____   _____

Who do you know? Family, friends, church, peers, career center people, alumni center people, former supervisors, fraternity/sorority, faculty, intern or job contacts—all need to be kept in contact to help you achieve your professional goals.

Practice

Write down new contacts the day you get them. Call them or e-mail them within a week to develop a relationship. Follow up from time to time to maintain the relationship.

Chapter 8

Adapt for Success

The employment world changes quickly, and those who have prepared themselves to succeed in a rapidly changing environment can use these changes to their advantage. The ability to seamlessly change to meet new conditions is called adaptability. When I was in college, the change from work being done on paper to computers was the biggest hurdle for professionals. Those who embraced this new technology were ahead of the game for a while, but as software changed, it continued to be critical to stay up with computer technology to succeed in any business. In academics, faculty used to depend on their grade book and their academic research notes. Now all records are submitted online and publishing research requires advanced computer skills. It doesn't matter how brilliant you are; if you don't understand the technology for the job, you won't be hired. Those who don't adapt to a changing workplace are forced to retire or to change jobs. Whatever the job, people who seek the latest ideas and technology show that they are adaptable and will have the best opportunities.

Unwritten Rules of Chapter 8:

Adaptability Is More Important Now Than Ever

Whether it is keeping up with technology or being ready and willing to take a new direction with your career, the world moves fast. Hard work, determination, and past experience don't always overcome modern obstacles. Those who train for new opportunities and look forward to new challenges are the ones most likely to be rewarded.

Adapt by Keeping Up with Technology

Most in-job changes that occur these days are related to technology. The bad news here is that technology is usually increased in order to decrease the total number of employees that a company needs. The good news is that the business will need employees who understand and can use the new technology, and they will also need to buy and maintain the systems that are incorporated and to train other people to use it. How can you stay up with changing technology? Here are some places that offer inexpensive classes or workshops: library centers, vocational or technical centers, evening or online classes from a college or junior college, or a workshop that is offered independently or from your existing job. Whether it is a free workshop or an online course, it is up to you to stay ahead. The time and money invested can lead to more opportunities and higher pay in the long run.

Adapt by Giving Yourself Options

I often hear very specific answers from students about their future employment. In general, it is good to know where you want to go in life, but one thing that many people don't know is that more than half of college graduates end up working in a different job than they trained for in college. Students may say, "I am going to own my own business" or "I am going to be a commercial architect," but what if this doesn't pan out right away? In order to deal the changing market conditions, it is best to give yourself as many options as possible. One modern adaptation is to double major in college. Here is an example:

Kellie was a premed student who planned to go to medical school and become a doctor. Along the way, she realized that she had a real interest in the environment. Fortunately, environmental science and premed had a lot of shared classes, so Kellie was able to double major without having to pay much extra and graduated on time. During her senior year, Kellie submitted applications to medical school and completed an internship in environmental science. In the end, she didn't get into the medical school she wanted, but she really enjoyed her internship and ended up taking a scientific job with a local health department. This allowed her to have a career that was related to human health with good pay and benefits right out of college.

Roll with the Punches

Another critical element of adaptability is to remain calm and patient when conditions change. There are cycles in life just as there are cycles in weather. There may be a giant storm today, but it will pass if you can ride it out. One of the best ways to get through trying times with a job is to give yourself other options. If you have another job possibility waiting, a lot of things get easier. First, you are not so afraid to speak up for your rights. Second, the leverage of another job can allow you to ask for better working conditions or a raise in salary. Third, keeping your options open can lead to better pay or a more exciting career in a new job. The corporate and service job markets see average turnover in jobs every three to four years. This means that if you start working at twenty and retire at sixty-five, you are likely to change titles or companies more than ten times! Hopefully most of those changes will be ones that you anticipate and control rather than layoffs that make you the victim of a surprise. Most employers understand these numbers, and they don't expect employees to be any more loyal than they are willing to be. If you stay calm in trying situations, the boss will be much more willing to write or call your new job with a strong reference that helps you get the job.

Be Willing to Move

Bill and John both began working as meteorologists for the National Weather Service in the same year. Both had outstanding work records, and they each put in for a promotion when they were eligible. Bill was promoted three times in the next ten years, while John was never promoted. John continued to apply for open positions, and despite having good qualifications, he never got the next job. He was still a journeyman when Bill became the head of his own office. What made the difference? Bill was willing to go anywhere. He put in applications to several places, went wherever the best job was offered, or the newest training was possible. John simply bid for jobs in his own office. He liked his house, his life, and his friends just the way they were, and he refused to consider moving in order to get a promotion. There is no rule disqualifying internal applications, but bosses in most businesses and even government agencies like to hire from outside and will not promote people beyond a certain point in-house. This gives a tremendous advantage to people who are willing to relocate.

Even if you are staying in your own region, it is good to expand the job search. Many beginning teachers don't find jobs immediately in the city where they want to work. What is their best option? They could stay in that town and do some substitute teaching or take a different type of job to get by, but neither of these options will get them real experience and references. The better choice is to take a job at a rural school or an urban school somewhere else and build up job experience. The time spent will be valuable personally and professionally, and when a job does open up where they want to be, then they have the experience to make a strong application and can move back to their favorite town.

It is a big world out there, and work opportunities can happen almost anywhere on the planet these days. Some Americans are still adapting to this idea. Embrace that experience, and take a chance on living and working in a new place. Seeing new places, meeting new people, and learning new ways to do things will all make you a well-rounded person and will be an exciting life experience as well. I know one former Drury University student who runs his own travel company in Bali, Indonesia. He takes people on six-week adventure treks into Papua New Guinea. He is making good money and having the time of his life. What adventure job or destination would you like to try?

Adapting for Fight or Flight

Animals in the wild are conditioned to decide in a split second whether they should choose fight or flight in a given situation. Things can be a lot more complicated for people and their careers. In order to have a quality life experience, however, the same skill needs to be applied to work. Mistakes can be made in either direction. For example, some people are constantly changing jobs because they claim they are not treated well by their boss or fellow employees. When this becomes a pattern, you have to consider that it is the employee, not the job, who is to blame. Many supervisors are like football coaches. They will purposely push you to test your limits of patience or productivity. If you pass the test, you have their loyalty and trust and can hopefully reap the benefits of this for a long time. If this test of your abilities and patience goes on too long, ask other employees how long the probation period is for this boss. If the answer is that you simply need to grin and bear it because that is just the way you will be treated here forever, it might be time to pack your bags and move on to another job.

Other people stay in jobs for years or even decades but complain that they don't like their job or don't respect their boss or colleagues. Considering that we average forty or more hours per week at our jobs, staying at a job that you really don't like is a big compromise in the quality of life and can even lead to depression or other serious problems. If the boss or employees at a job are simply abusive or the job or business itself simply doesn't match your values at all, it is time to go. Most people eventually find the job that best matches their interests and needs and then say good-bye to the job that isn't right for them.

Adaptability Quiz

		True	False
1.	Being adaptable means solving problems on your own.	____	____
2.	Training for different careers makes you adaptable.	____	____
3.	When tested at a new job, you should quit and move on.	____	____
4.	Attitude can be the most important factor in adaptability.	____	____
5.	Good networking makes you more adaptable.	____	____
6.	Being adaptable now means giving up your long-term dream.	____	____
7.	Staying up with technology is a key to adaptability.	____	____
8.	Continuing education isn't needed if you have a job.	____	____
9.	Louder and more assertive people are better at adapting to changing conditions.	____	____
10.	Your potential employer will want you to be adaptable.	____	____

Answers to the Adaptability Quiz

1. False. Independence is good in some situations, but in a business setting, it is best to utilize the people around you. They have valuable experience to share and can usually help you solve problems more efficiently and quickly than you could on your own.

2. True. The more different options you give yourself, the more likely you will be in a satisfying career right away. Most people don't get their dream job the first time around, but that is OK. The life and work experiences in other jobs along the way will lead to a strong list of references and accomplishments that will ultimately lead to the dream job.

3. False. Quitting a job at the first sign of challenge can be a big mistake. Almost all jobs have a probationary period, but the ways to pass it are usually not told to new employees. It is up to you to ask those who have been through the process how to get past this test and to ask if it is worth the effort.

4. True. Attitude is critical when adapting to new situations. Just like emergency situations, important decisions and actions on the job are best accomplished by staying calm and having a positive attitude. Fighting with people or fighting against changes in the workplace will lead to problems with supervisors and fellow employees.

5. True. Networking is the way to get a new job or to get your dream job. The more people you have in your active network, the more people you have keeping their eyes out for your next opportunity. This makes you more adaptable because you have more opportunities to choose from, whether it is your first job or a better job.

6. False. Careers often take interesting twists and turns, but most people say that the experiences in between each helped them prepare for their dream job. Being open to new experiences or jobs that are outside the direct track line you have chosen can help build your résumé and expand your list of valuable contacts. Along the way, people often realize that what they originally thought was

going to be their dream job is really not for them. Along the way, they have found a different passion or better pay and benefits, which cause them to redefine their dream job altogether.

7. True. No matter the job or the training for the next job, it is critical to do the work to keep up with technology. It may be boring, and it may even cost you money, but this investment in time and cash will pay off with more job offers, better job offers, and more frequent promotions.

8. False. Thanks (or no thanks) to technology moving so rapidly, prejob and on-the-job training are a continuous necessity. Some of this can be done online, some can be done at work, and other times a conference workshop or professional class will need to be taken. Be sure to list this training and any certificates that have been earned on your résumé. Just remember, even if you are doing your job well, if you don't stay up with professional advances, you will be out-of-date as a person or as a business in about three years.

9. False. It is the calm, quiet people with a positive attitude who usually have an advantage in adapting to changing situations. These people are watching and listening, and they are better prepared to know who to ask to help solve a problem or where to go if they need to look for a new job. In addition to this, calm people don't burn bridges. Even though they may change jobs, they have a good working relationship with their peers and their boss. People want to help them succeed because they like them. That means that they will get good assistance and strong references that will help in the long run.

10. True. Employers themselves need to be more adaptable than ever these days. Suppliers, customers, and costs can all change rapidly, and they need employers who can adapt quickly to these changing conditions. Whether it is industry, education, business, or a service industry, the ability to do several things well makes you a more valuable commodity to employers. People who can only do one thing well are often called one-trick ponies and are at risk of being let go in hard times if someone else can do their job plus serve other functions as well.

Review

1. Adapt by keeping up with technology. The research takes time, and computer and phone upgrades are an investment in your own future.

2. Adapt by giving yourself options. There are many possible careers out there that might be rewarding for you. Consider what your second and third choices might be, and prepare for them with specific training.

3. Adapt by utilizing the people around you. Don't bang your head against a door; someone nearby probably has the key to that door and can let you in.

4. Roll with the punches. If you stay calm, most things that initially seem like big problems will become small problems or even go away on their own.

5. Adapt by being willing to move to new places and try new things in order to reach personal and professional rules.

6. Adapt for fight or flight. Are you being tested or abused? A test demands a fight, but it is best to get out of a situation where you are being abused.

Self-Evaluation

Rate yourself from 1 to 10 on adaptability. Use the space provided to explain why you gave yourself this rating.

Adaptability _____ _____

When faced with a "no" or other obstacle, how good is your strategy to adapt, change directions, or overcome?

Practice

Use a five-part strategy to deal with an obstacle, remembering that most obstacles are people, ideas, or the interpretation of rules:

1. Take a deep breath, and consider your options.
2. Consult with someone who may have an objective opinion on your situation.
3. Stay calm and use determination to find a way over, under, or around the obstacle.
4. Be prepared to change course if the obstacle can't be overcome.
5. Be willing to move to a new place or a new job. Some companies will not promote people in one location but require a move (even if they don't say this). Other times, there isn't a job opening where you want it right now. In this case, it is definitely better to begin your career somewhere other than your dream destination, and take a promotion to move there later.

How to Adapt to Obstacles Put in Your Way

Beyond obvious physical changes in a work environment, like the change to computers, I have found that another critical element is the mental approach to problems. Here is one example:

Adapting to Obstacles: Example 1

Imagine that you are in an office. This is a typical office on the third floor of a building. It has windows and has ceiling tiles that cover a crawl space. You need to get into the office next door in five minutes for a legitimate reason, but the door to that office is closed and locked. What do you do?

Use the space below, and give yourself five minutes to write an answer.

Adapting to Obstacles: Example 2

Consider that you need one more class to graduate, but the class is full. The professor says there is no space left. You don't want to have to spend another semester and more money to complete one more class. What can you do?

Use the space below, and give yourself five minutes to write an answer.

Answer to Example 1. Getting into the office next door.

Here are some of the answers I have received in the past.

1. Climb out the window, crawl along the ledge, and get into the window in the next office.
2. Climb up to the ceiling, pop out a ceiling tile, and crawl over to the next office, then drop down inside it.
3. Break out the window or kick in the door of the office.

While these options might physically get you into the office, they also put you at risk of injury or legal problems.

Here are some better answers:

1. Call or knock on the door even though it is locked. The person who works there may be inside and let you in.
2. Find the nearest administrative assistant and ask if they have a master key to let you in.
3. Call security and explain the situation and ask for them to let you in.

Adapt by Utilizing the People Around You

The key point of this exercise is to get people to realize that we have been taught by school and our parents to become more independent, but that the work environment rewards us more for being dependent. No single person knows the answers to everything, but someone else nearby probably does. The people who are confident enough to incorporate the knowledge and experience of people around them will be much more adaptable to new situations than those who stubbornly try to solve every problem on their own.

Answers to Example 2. Overcoming when someone tells you that you can't do something.

Here are some common mistakes I have witnessed related to overcoming a personal or administrative obstacle:

1. Lose your temper and demand satisfaction from the other person.
2. Simply say OK, walk away, and accept the consequences.
3. Immediately go over the head of the person who has said no to you before calmly explaining your situation face-to-face in order to show them that you are a responsible person and will do a good job for them.

Here are strategies that work when trying to overcome an administrative obstacle:

1. Stay calm, check all the rules, and try to appeal to the logic and the emotions of the other person to help you.
2. Never give up until all avenues have been exhausted. In this case, even if the professor never lets you into the class, there may be an online class that could be taken or an independent study offered by a different professor. There are almost always many more ways to get things done than you think.
3. Once a face-to-face appeal has failed, go to the next higher administrator and appeal to them. They are not personally vested in the outcome, and they want to resolve problems as quickly as possible. They have seen these situations many times before and know how to solve them.

Chapter 9

Remember, Every Word Matters

Many of our initial impressions are made through writing, followed up by interviews where we give verbal answers. Whether it is an introductory e-mail, letter of application, or résumé, our writing quality and speaking proficiency make a huge difference. One of the biggest hurdles for young people is that they are used to communicating by texting or other hurried writing styles. This leads to slang, abbreviations, and poor spelling. Even some high-level professionals, such as college faculty, doctors, or corporate managers, can get lazy with their writing. This chapter provides some tips on how to be a high-quality and effective writer and speaker.

Unwritten Rules of Chapter 9:

Good Communication Is Always Noticed

1. New hires and students are of a different generation than supervisors and professors. In order for the two to communicate, they must avoid the slang and jargon (and popular references to movies and music as well) and get right to the point. From the introductory e-mail to a face-to-face interview, effective communication is critical.
2. The first and last paragraphs of a job proposal or a college paper should be equally strong. Many professor and businesspeople skip to the conclusions first. If the conclusions are weak, they won't spend much time on the rest of the paper. Usually, if the ending is strong, the whole piece of writing is strong as well.

Avoid Slang Terms

Even if everyone in the country seems to be saying something a certain way, slang makes you sound less professional. Be sure to avoid cute or common terms and stick with the professional, formal terms for everything. Even more discouraging are the habit words that can creep into your language and then end up in your writing. When I first began teaching, I was so anxious for feedback that I ended each sentence with "OK?" I didn't even notice until someone told me, and then I didn't believe it until I videotaped one of my lectures and watched it myself. It took some time, but I was able to break that habit. Now I am careful to get feedback and record my work from time to time to be sure that the communication is effective.

I recently had a conversation about a similar problem with a very talented young woman. Both in conversation and in her e-mails, she had allowed the word "like" to sneak in constantly. It so dominated each sentence that the value of the content was being totally lost. I knew that she was getting ready to graduate and had set up several interviews, so I recommended that she practice interview with the career center staff and have them record the practice sessions. Fortunately, she was able to break this habit, and thanks to a great transcript and a strong interview, she landed a job with the Federal Reserve.

Get to the Point

Professional writing is quite a bit different from scholarly writing. Students often feel that the more they write, the better their grade will be. A coworker, boss, or potential employer wants written material to be as brief as possible and wants the most important materials to be at the very front. I found this out while working in Washington, DC, for National Geographic Society. We were trying to secure federal funding for geography education and had been requested to meet with each congressperson from our state. My state is Missouri, so I had requested and ended up confirming six meetings with senators and representatives. National Geographic Society hired Patton Boggs, a prestigious law firm, to help us prepare our request materials. They asked us to describe our state geography education history, programs, and funding needs. Then they said that it had to fit on one page. My education organization was twenty years old, so listing all our accomplishments and needs initially surpassed five pages. Once we looked through it and considered exactly what we were trying to accomplish, it became clear that a couple of examples of high-level accomplishments, along with a list of budgeted needs, were all that were needed. When we actually met with our members of congress, they typically looked at our page, talked to us for about five minutes, and then decided whether to support the legislation or not. If top people in the US government spend this little time and effort on national education policy, consider how little time might be spent reviewing your next written request. Make your point quickly, strongly, and with supportive evidence. If more is needed, you can always add to it later upon request.

Edit, Edit, Edit

Most people realize that they should edit reports or their résumés or applications, but they forget the most common type of writing of all: e-mail. Sometimes, an e-mail is an extremely important document. It can be a first contact, a follow-up request, or a work necessity, but the quality of the writing is important no matter what the application. People are judging the content and the quality of the writing, so be sure to look it over thoroughly, and whenever possible, have someone else look at it as well before you hit the Send button. One big mistake that people make is to craft a good e-mail that is supposed to include an attachment, such as a résumé, and then they forget to add the attachment. This is not just embarrassing, but it can lead to your name going farther down the list of potential candidates. Sometimes, it is even best to wait overnight and then edit an e-mail the next day before sending it. If you are angry, sad, distracted, or excited, it is very likely that there will be mistakes or even the wrong tone conveyed in the message. Waiting until the next day and editing can usually catch these problems.

Research until All Points Are Justified

Besides group work, the number one complaint by college students is that they get tired of writing research papers. Most of them understand that research and writing are good for them, but they still don't like it (just like my children don't like to eat their broccoli). The students who enjoy research and take the time to do it right end up standing out like shooting stars by comparison to the average, lazy effort. Research, even academic research, is easier now than it has ever been. If you know how to search, most answers can be found online from anywhere in the world. The only problem is that searching online can be extremely inefficient, and the quality of the findings can vary tremendously. The key is to follow links until you are sure you have reached the original, legitimate source, the primary source as it is known. If you don't know how to do this, a reference librarian can help you learn. Some people forget that there is a live, free, experienced person who gets paid to help you learn how to become better at research. Investing an hour of your time to walk into the library and ask this person for help can set you up for a lifetime of successful research. After that, it is a matter of practicing to get better and faster at locating key facts or ideas. A few years back, I hired a young woman who was so good at online research that she seemed to be able to find answers before I even finished asking the question. The research skill developed by this young woman led to exactly the job she wanted: a grant-writing career for a nonprofit environmental organization.

Reach a Strong Conclusion

Perhaps even more common than poor research in writing is a lack of strong conclusions. If people are going to read to the end of something, such as a work proposal or an application letter, they expect a logical summary with strong critical-thinking skills to be found in the conclusion. Consider an application letter. Why would the employer hire you or a committee give you a scholarship rather than someone else? Every applicant will have basically the same qualifications. Applicants often separate themselves with the last paragraph of their application. How convincing are they at demonstrating that they have the strongest skills to do this job? How clearly do they show their passion for this type of work? How do they combine research understanding of the position with personal discussion of why taking this job is a good fit for the company and for their own professional goals? Whether it is a research paper, job application, college application, or grant proposal, the research summary and personal evaluation found on the last page or in the last paragraph often separates the winners from the losers.

Every Word Matters Quiz

		True	False
1.	It is OK to abbreviate or use slang.	_____	_____
2.	People expect to find typos in e-mails.	_____	_____
3.	It is best to wait and edit before sending an e-mail.	_____	_____
4.	Applications and papers should be as long as possible.	_____	_____
5.	Online encyclopedias are a good place to find research data.	_____	_____
6.	Reference librarians want to help you get better at research.	_____	_____
7.	Use it or lose it; you need to practice research.	_____	_____
8.	Young students and employees are not respected for their conclusions.	_____	_____
9.	Good conclusions must summarize and give personal observations.	_____	_____
10.	The last paragraph is not very important when selecting applicants.	_____	_____

Answers to the Every Word Matters Quiz

1. False. All professional communication should be formal in style, straight to the point, and as short as humanly possible (in full sentences).

2. False. People are always evaluating you. They might not be surprised to find a typo, but you can bet that they will attribute it to sloppy, unprofessional work on your part.

3. True. If I have a student, faculty member, or administrator who makes me angry, I write the e-mail, but don't edit or send it until the next day. The same goes for an extremely important e-mail such as one that has an application attached. It is also best to have someone else look at it so they can catch any typo or improper tone that might have been put there unconsciously by you.

4. False. Whether it is a professor or an employer, more pages written by you equals more work for them. The writing sample must meet all required elements, but once that is done, keep the document as short as possible out of respect for the person who has to read it.

5. False. Online encyclopedias may have some correct answers, but they are not primary sources. It is all right to begin a search at this type of site, but it is critical to follow up all the way to the verified, original source to be sure that what you have is real research and not fiction, opinion, or worse.

6. True. Don't be afraid of the library. It is more efficient the first time to have a real live person show you how to find something than to spend hours or days finding it on your own. Reference librarians wouldn't exist without customers, so it is job security for them to help you.

7. True. The online sources of data are constantly changing, and the search engines to find them are always evolving as well. The only way to keep up and to get faster at research is to practice it.

8. False. Good employers and faculty pay especially close attention to the last section of an application or paper. Employers want to know that the person they are hiring will make a valuable contribution. They want a problem solver, and the conclusion demonstrates both organization and critical thinking skills. In the long term, the better one's employees are at solving problems, the fewer problems will have to be faced by the boss.

9. True. It is critical for a conclusion to summarize the most important points and then add the personal information that can show that you can research well, summarize even better, and can evaluate things in a logical, efficient, and creative way.

10. False. Some scholarship committees skip directly to the conclusions. The rest of the application is so similar that it can't be used to decide who is best qualified. Many employers use this trick as well, so always be sure that the last paragraph gets the most attention, is very focused, and makes sense on its own.

Review

1. Don't use slang or habit words.

2. Get to the point.

3. Edit, edit, edit. Mistakes are unprofessional. They will cost you a job.

4. Research until all points are justified. Strong, primary research shows a mastery of the material at hand and will separate your work from others.

5. Reach a strong conclusion. Managers often read the conclusion first. If it doesn't tell them everything they need to know in summary, they don't read the rest.

Self-Evaluation

Rate your own writing and speaking style from 1 to 10. Use the space below to explain why you gave yourself this rating.

Writing and Speaking

Whether it is an effective e-mail, application, or grant proposal, every job requires good writing. To be hired or to make a presentation, good speaking skills are required as well.

Overall quality   _____   _____

Research skills   _____   _____

Analysis skills   _____   _____

Practice Speaking

How do you know if you are using too much slang? Record yourself during a normal conversation with a friend, and then play it back. In five minutes, you will notice how many more slang terms you use in conversation than you thought. Have the friend write up an interview list, and then record this session as well. Continue practicing until you are comfortable that the style and content of the language you are using matches the interview or presentation style you need.

Practice Writing

There are many ways to improve writing. The most important is to write a draft, then revise to a working copy, and then edit for a final version. At the working copy stage, you should consult a peer or professional to review your work, make sure it is on target, and assist with editing. Give yourself plenty of time to add additional resources, receive feedback, and to make a strong final edit, and your future writing projects will be outstanding work.

Chapter 10

Use Electronic Communication the Right Way

Academic and business communications are the fastest and easiest that they have ever been. We can stay in touch, ask questions, receive documents, and have video chats from anywhere with electronic devices. We can keep up with work or research real-time information with Facebook and Twitter. All of these tools are useful, and we need to be familiar with them to succeed in the modern workplace. Unfortunately, the speed and the informal nature of these communications can also get us into big trouble if they are not used professionally.

Here is one recent example. I received the following e-mail from a female student:

> Subject line: Dr. Terry, I can't find my pants!

This e-mail was cc'd to several other students, any of whom could have forwarded the e-mail to the dean of the college or my wife with no explanation given for this strange and possibly damaging e-mail. In real life, there was no problem here. My wife and I had escorted a group of students to Washington, DC, for a conference. One of them had left a pair of pants in her room and didn't know how to get them back. I recommended she call the hotel, and they gladly shipped them back at no charge. Fortunately there was no damage done in this case, but hopefully, you can see how important it is to be very careful with the wording of e-mails. You never know where they might go or how they could be misunderstood and come back to haunt you.

Unwritten Rules of Chapter 10:

Every Word Matters in an E-mail

Whether it is the words in the subject line, the words used in the introduction, or the total number of words in the text, every word matters in an e-mail. People sometimes read e-mails when they are tired or in a bad mood. This affects how they may interpret the language that you write. If anything in the e-mail is unclear, the other person may misunderstand and react badly to it. Poorly written e-mails waste time and are disrespectful to the people who have to read them. If you write and edit them correctly the first time, e-mail will be one of your most valuable tools.

Use E-mail, but Do It Thoughtfully

E-mail is a tool that makes group work much easier. Attaching files, photos, and messages to each group member can easily keep everyone in the loop no matter where they are. E-mail also allows you to add the supervisor to the conversation so they can stay updated on the progress. These are all great reasons to use e-mail to advance a project, and I require my students to keep in touch and keep me updated this way.

Use Facebook and Twitter that Mom Could See

It is often suggested that the faculty look at some of their student's Facebook or Twitter posts to get a better idea of who they are. It is widely known that employers do the same thing. As an employer, the Facebook and Twitter postings of young people can be pretty frightening. Many post photos while they are intoxicated, often using profanity and containing links to raunchy or even perverse websites. I have even seen students use very revealing or provocative photos as their profile photo. Now I will readily admit that I am not a prude and believe young people should have fun, but if I were the potential employer, this type of behavior might help me select the people I would want to interview and those I would not. Once posts of words, photos, or videos are up on the web, anyone may end up with them. With that in mind, even at my age, before I post something, I ask myself, "Would my mom be OK with this?" If the answer is yes, then it is probably OK for anyone to see it.

Be Efficient with E-Communications

Both Facebook and Twitter are becoming even more important as society learns how to use these tools to better communicate and stay up-to-date. In fact, in a recent poll, nearly half of those asked said that they used social media on their phone to keep up with severe weather warnings rather than the traditional media. Social media has even been given credit as helping to support the Arab Spring democracy movements of the Middle East region in 2011. Despite all their useful qualities, it is easy to end up wasting large amounts of time with them. How can you avoid this? Be sure to dedicate a specific amount of time each day for professional and personal e-mail and social-media time. Stick to this time as religiously as you can. Don't get caught up feeling that you need to reply to every tweet, posting, or e-mail as they happen. It may be a fast-moving world, but some things can wait. As a matter of fact, I have found that some things will resolve on their own if I don't respond immediately. If it isn't urgent, let it wait until the time you have specified to work on it, and then take care of all the communications at once. This will save you time and effort throughout the week.

Electronic Communication Quiz

		True	False
1.	Humor should never be used in business e-mails.	————	————
2.	The more e-mails and texts, the better you communicate.	————	————
3.	If an e-mail makes you upset, respond immediately.	————	————
4.	Informality in e-mails shows confidence.	————	————
5.	Subject lines in e-mails are important.	————	————
6.	You should learn to use Facebook and Twitter.	————	————
7.	People can't see my private Facebook pages.	————	————
8.	There should be a scheduled time for e-communication.	————	————
9.	Reply All usually saves time with e-mails.	————	————
10.	Short e-mails are better than long e-mails.	————	————

Answers to the Electronic Communication Quiz

1. True. Humor can be used in person. It can only hurt you in a professional e-mail. People have different senses of humor, and what is funny to you may be offensive to others.

2. False. One of the easiest ways to get people to lose interest is to give them an avalanche of communication. If you limit the communication to only that which is important and necessary, then people will pay attention and follow up on it.

3. False. Whenever possible, call or speak to someone in person if an e-mail makes you upset. This will help avoid conflict. If you must e-mail, wait a day to respond and have someone look at the e-mail before you hit Send.

4. False. Informality in e-mails is more likely to show disrespect than to show confidence.

5. True. People decide whether or not to read an e-mail based on the subject line. Usually, it is the only part of the e-mail that you can guarantee they see. With that in mind, it needs to be sure to say the right thing and not have a chance to be misinterpreted. For that reason, "Dr. Terry, I can't find my pants," is not the best subject line.

6. True. Most young people today already know how to use social media. The best part is that social media is getting even stronger, faster, and more useful every year. It is a critical tool for success as long as it is used correctly.

7. False. Security settings may change, and links to you may be made through friends, family, or references. It is naive to believe that you can post controversial things and that they will never leave your personal friend network.

8. True. Without a strict time schedule, you can waste a whole day tinkering around with e-mail, Facebook, or Twitter. Limit your time, and you will get more done.

9. False. Reply All is only for group work or special circumstances. It will usually not save any time. As a matter of fact, I recently had one colleague who hit Reply All with a humorous take on the previous e-mail and lost the whole next day because of it. As it turns out, his e-mail was offensive to quite a few people, and he spent the next day apologizing to the whole e-mail list and making calls to individuals to correct for this mistake.

10. True. Short e-mails are effective. Long e-mails test the patience of the reader. There needs to be just enough detail for the person on the other end to fully understand your e-mail. After that, any additional comments or questions will be lost or ignored.

Review

1. E-mail, but do it thoughtfully. Make every word matter, and don't send too many e-mails.

2. Use Facebook and Twitter that mom could see. Electronic communication could come back to haunt you, so avoid controversial statements or photos.

3. Be efficient with e-communication. Electronic communication is a great tool, but don't let it take over your life. If you aren't careful, it can waste large amounts of time.

Self-Evaluation

Rate yourself between 1 to 10 on electronic communication. Use the space provided to explain why you have given this rating.

E-communication

How effectively do you use e-mail and social media?

—— _____

Practice

Utilize these important guidelines to use when writing an e-mail.

1. The first is to be very brief and to the point in e-mails. Don't bury your questions or answers in paragraphs of text, and don't send out ten different e-mails per day. If you do this, people will lose focus before they finish the e-mail and may not respond to all or part of it. Try to ask only one question, and make sure it is easy to find at the top.
2. It is also extremely important not to make any personal comments or attempt any jokes or other humor on e-mail. E-mails have the dangerous potential to be used against you, so make sure you edit each e-mail before sending it to be sure that it is clear, correct, and politically acceptable.
3. Have a colleague or friend preview the e-mail if you have any concerns about its content. If attachments are part of the process, be sure everyone is using the same software formats so that photos and text will be able to be combined seamlessly in the end.
4. Don't e-mail when you're angry. If you are responding to something that made you angry, wait a day and then calmly write a reply. If at all possible, respond in person or on the phone to be sure that your response is clearly understood. If you must reply by e-mail, keep the reply very neutral and simple, not personal.

Always be sure to have someone else preview this type of e-mail to avoid inflaming the conversation.

5. Avoid using Reply All unless absolutely necessary. The more people there are to read the e-mail, the more chances that someone will misunderstand all or part of it.

6. Be formal and use good grammar. E-mail may be the first impression you make and often includes important requests. You will gain respect and get better results if you treat e-mails accordingly. Use the person's title (in my case, Dr. Terry), and write out the complete idea. Introductions that begin with "Hey" are only for friends or family.

Chapter 11

Critical Thinking:
It's More Critical than You Think

How good are you at thinking? We measure it to a limited extent with exams in school, but that method doesn't give us the whole picture. Some people who score poorly on exams are quite good at thinking on their feet. This is why most job interviews are conducted in person (or at least with a videoconference). Employers want to know how quickly you can respond to questions and how effectively you can solve problems and then communicate the solution to others. This chapter contains tips to becoming better at critical thinking.

Unwritten Rules of Chapter 11:

Success Comes from Creative Living and Creative Listening

1. Just as individuals need to be adaptable these days, businesses and even colleges need to have fresh ideas as well. They are looking for creative solutions from students and new hires. There are many ways to feed your creative side, from attending a museum gallery opening to taking a hike in a natural environment. It is good to try new things so that you can see new things, meet new people, and challenge your mind in new ways. Feeding your creative side will relax you, add more meaning to recreational time, and provide creative inspiration to your work as well.

2. New ideas come from listening. People learn by listening. Most of us know when it is time to let other people talk, but few of us

are really listening. Take the time to dig deeper and let the other person explain why they feel a certain way and how they come up with new ideas. Not only will they like you more, you will learn about them and probably about a lot of other important things as well.

Feed Your Creative Side

Many of us have been conditioned to believe that the time we spend with recreational reading, visiting an art gallery, or attending a science fiction movie is purely free time. I argue that this time can be extremely productive. Here are three reasons why: First, when we are stumped by a difficult problem, our conscious mind has a tendency to lock up. At this point, we can sit there trying to figure out the problem all night, but nothing happens. We can often jump-start this process by distracting the conscious mind with another pleasant activity. Once the active mind is reading or watching TV, our unconscious mind can go to work and solve our problem.

Second, exposing ourselves to new people can lead to answers from unexpected places. I was conducting research in Hawaii one time and had noticed in the paper that there was a big outcry against the new Superferry docking in Lahaina Harbor. Surprisingly, I found the answer to the public concern when I stepped into a knife shop. The curator mentioned that the ferry was in town, and when I asked why people were upset, it turned out that this knife shop owner was also a PhD in marine biology and knew all about it. I certainly didn't go into that shop to find an answer, but the answer came anyway, solving a problem for me and reminding me that the people around us often have much more knowledge than we give them credit.

Third, looking at a piece of art, listening to a piece of music, or reading a new book can all expand our life experience. This allows us to consider problems from different angles and creative new outlooks. So next time your friends are stuck on a problem and plan to pull an all-nighter to solve it, step out for a couple of hours for creative time. Chances are you will come back with better options than the people who stayed at the desk, blindly hoping for inspiration to arrive.

Be Open to New Ideas

Humans are like a pyramid when it comes to accepting new ideas. When we are young, the base is wide. We are very creative, making our own music, drawing, painting, and openly listening to those around us in order to learn how the world works. Once we get older and have found out some things that work, we tend to start closing down our worldview. By the time we reach retirement, most people don't want to hear about other people's opinions or learn new ways to improve their job. The only way that older companies stay in business is to hire open-minded young professionals to inject that needed creativity back into their business. You may have heard that many colleges and businesses have been actively trying to incorporate "diversity" in recent years. This is not, as many people believe, simply an affirmative action plan. It is a survival plan, and no matter what your race or gender is, you can take advantage of it.

Ask yourself the following questions to test your own open-mindedness.

1. Do I consider the race of the person before I listen to their suggestion?
2. Do I consider the gender of the person before I take them seriously?
3. If someone has a different idea than mine to solve a problem, do I dismiss their idea initially, thinking mine must be better?
4. Do I feel out of control if I am not in charge?
5. Am I uncomfortable going outside the box to find answers?
6. Am I uncomfortable working with people from other countries with foreign accents?

If you can honestly answer no to the questions posed above, then you will have a tremendous advantage when it comes to being hired. Every business is now on global interests, so they want to hire people who are open to working with all types of people and who are comfortable with the possibility of travel for professional development.

Be Mr. Spock

The original *Star Trek* series on TV and in movies had two very different stars: Captain Kirk and Mr. Spock. Captain Kirk was in charge of the starship, and Mr. Spock was his first officer. What made them a great team was that Captain Kirk used his instincts, his emotion, and his boundless enthusiasm to solve problems. Mr. Spock, on the other hand, claimed to have no emotions and solved each problem based on science, mathematics, and other logical means. When Captain Kirk's ideas didn't make sense, Mr. Spock had the courage to point it out in a calm and reasoned way.

Most people relate much more to Captain Kirk because like him, we are all creatures of emotion. Working on instinct doesn't take research; it is spontaneous and therefore is much more fun than the logical approach. On the other hand, there is a great deal more risk involved in taking an emotional approach versus the logical one. Consider if these two were to go into a casino. Captain Kirk would bet based on emotion and competitive spirit. He would probably use a high-risk strategy trying to make a big score. He might be up for a while, but the mathematical odds of gambling would eventually catch up, and his competitive nature wouldn't allow him to leave until he had lost some or all his investment. Mr. Spock probably would know better than to invest any money gambling, but if he went into the casino, he would know that the best odds are at craps or blackjack. He would also know that on average, people who really know the numbers can get to about double their money on many nights, and if they simply pick up their winnings at this point and go home, they will make up for most of the times when they simply lose.

Whether it is during a conversation or launching a new business, be sure to present yourself as a logical person who has numbers and research on their side of the argument. Overly emotional people make other people nervous and can be inconsistent with their productivity. Being a logical candidate will make hiring you seem like a low-risk and potential high-reward investment for an employer. If it is appropriate, there will be plenty of time to show off your more instinctive and flamboyant side later.

Be a Good Listener

I once wrote down a list of my favorite people in the world and the people who had been the most influential in my life. Included on this list were my parents, my family doctor, one restaurant manager, my best friend and his father, my PhD advisor, a college-teaching mentor, and my first boss as a professor. I looked at this list for a while, trying to understand what separated these people from the thousands of other people I had met through the years. Eventually it hit me: each of these people had asked me important questions, really listened to my answers, and then encouraged me in positive directions toward success. What an amazing discovery! Whether you are a student, a new employee, or even the boss, being a good listener is an extremely important skill.

Think about the people whom you respect and trust the most in life. I am sure that they will fit the good-listener profile as well. Unfortunately, I was not born a good listener. The fact that I make my living by talking in classrooms is not an accident. I like to talk, but talking is not the best way to learn the basics of something. When it came to my early jobs, I simply tried to get by on working hard and doing my own job well. There is nothing wrong with this, but it can end up in a lot of wasted time. If you listen well during training, for example, you will learn the best and most efficient way to do things. In addition to this, if you ask some more questions, you can also learn about the local politics: who to ask for help and who to avoid. People like to fill up silence, so remaining quiet also gives you power. If you ask an uncomfortable but important question and simply wait for the answer to come, it usually will. If you ask good questions during a job interview, it allows the boss to talk about his or her own philosophy on things, which gives you valuable information and gives them a comfort zone within the meeting. These days, whether I am discussing a class schedule with a student or a research grant with the president of the university, I always try to spend more time asking questions and listening than talking.

Listening is just as important with peers as it is with the boss. It is a simple matter of trust and respect. It is best to begin with the idea that the other person has a valid reason for believing something different than you and ask the questions that will allow you to understand the similarities and differences in their position versus yours. In the end, it doesn't really matter whether you agree with their opinion or not. You simply need to let them know that you respect their views and are willing to take the time to listen to them. Religious and political views can be the most contentious when it comes to this kind of discussion. While I encourage you to avoid these topics at work whenever possible, a logical, respectful listener will stay out of trouble, while those people who go out of their way to advertise their beliefs as the only truth will make enemies.

Critical Thinking Quiz

	True	False

1. The best way to learn about work politics is from the job description.   _____   _____

2. Going to an art museum is an inefficient use of time.   _____   _____

3. Reading a fiction novel can help you solve a problem.   _____   _____

4. You need to agree with what other people say in order to show respect for them.   _____   _____

5. It is best to explain all that you know in a job interview.   _____   _____

6. You can talk too much, but you can't listen too much.   _____   _____

7. Being too emotional puts you at risk.   _____   _____

8. Knowing the numbers behind an answer makes you a nerd.   _____   _____

9. An open mind means looking for contacts in unusual settings.   _____   _____

10. "Diversity hire" means limited opportunity for applicants.   _____   _____

Answers to the Critical Thinking Quiz

1. False. The best way to learn about work politics is to ask experienced people about it and then listen carefully to their responses. This is a case where who you know can really be more important than what you know.

2. False. Going out to an art museum puts you in contact with people and ideas and gives you a little exercise as well. All of these things can help to get your mind to relax and come back to work refreshed and with new ideas.

3. True. Whether it is a unique idea that you see in the novel or the simple distraction that lets your subconscious solve your problem, reading or any other pleasant distraction can be a productive problem-solving time.

4. False. Most people don't require that you agree with them. They simply want their ideas and feelings to be given equal merit and time with yours in the conversation.

5. False. It would be impossible to try to explain all you know in a meeting or job interview. Besides being impossible, it would also be extremely boring for the other person. Can you imagine having to sit through twenty interviews where applicants simply sat down and rattled on about their thoughts on a job for thirty minutes or an hour? That would be a mind-numbing experience for the people conducting the interview. It is best to give logical answers while being sure to ask important questions to the other person or people in the room.

6. True. I have been guilty of talking too much and never of listening too much. The only exception may be when a talented employee or student has a valuable contribution to make but stays silent. I see this sometimes when a student writes a brilliant paper but doesn't defend this strong research information in class when other students are debating the material. In this case, the student

hasn't listened too much, but they need to realize when their contribution is valuable and speak up.

7. True. Working on emotion is a roller coaster. Riding the highs and lows of emotion can lead to conflicts with other employees, as well as peaks and valleys in productivity levels. There are legitimate times to use your instincts, but it is also best to try to research the potential outcome in the numbers before following through with them.

8. False. Knowing the numbers behind an answer makes you prepared. This may lead to lazy employees or lazy students calling you a nerd, but that is not nearly as important as the boss or professor calling them lazy. When it comes to promotions or reference letters, the person who backs up what they say with good data will win out.

9. True. People are more complex than we often give them credit. I once had a tenant in my rental house turn me on to the pollution problems in the North Pacific gyre. I mentioned that I taught a resource management class, and he asked me if I had heard about all the plastic trash that was trapped and floating in the Pacific Ocean. This was useful information that I researched and developed into field projects for my students on a field trip to Hawaii. How did this man know about pollution in the North Pacific gyre? As it turned out, he was a retired naval intelligence officer and had sailed through that zone and seen it firsthand. Valuable information can come from nearly anyone or anywhere. Being open-minded and asking questions allow you to tap into these hidden reserves of information.

10. False. Just because a company says they are looking for diversity doesn't mean that they are narrowly looking to hire only one race or gender. White people get particularly upset with this term because they are defensive about being the majority (for now) in America, and thus they assume that they will be excluded from consideration in the hiring process. In most cases, employers' vested interest is in hiring the most qualified person regardless

of race, gender, or ethnicity. If candidates are equal, diversity often means that you bring something new, especially creative ideas to a company. Given this definition, a white candidate could bring diversity to a mostly black company just as well as a black worker could bring diversity to a business that has an all-white workforce. The key here is to listen to what the job requires and use good examples to show that you are trained to work with all kinds of people and have strong skills and ideas to bring to the table.

Review

1. Feed your creative side. Everything from recreational reading to meeting new people can lead to new ideas and new contacts.

2. Be open to new ideas. Accept that there are reasons for why people disagree, and try to sincerely understand the other side.

3. Be Mr. Spock. It is safer and more productive to follow logic rather than emotion.

4. Be a good listener. Don't just give people time to talk; try to listen to what they say and what they mean. This skill is equally important for the boss as it is for the first-year intern.

Self-Evaluation

Rate your creative ability from 1 to 10. Explain why you give this rating in the space provided.

Creativity   _____ _____

Thought "I have a new idea for that" or "I could have done that"? Everyone has the potential to be creative. What do you build into your life to relax, meet new people, or find inspiration? Art, music, recreational reading, and even hiking in nature can all ease the stress on the quantitative side of the brain and allow us to solve problems in new and creative ways.

Open to new ideas   _____ _____

Are you a good listener? It not only helps you learn, it shows respect to others.

Use of logic   _____ _____

Do you make decisions based on logical assumptions or quick, emotional responses? How effectively can you explain your logic to others?

Practice Creativity

It may seem strange to practice creativity, but where do ideas really come from? They often come from inspiration that follows contact to art, literature, or ideas that are on a totally different subject. Sometimes we just need to get some free time so that our subconscious can solve problems for us. To practice, try to read something new, go someplace new, or meet someone new at least once per week. Not only will you feed your creative side, you will be having fun and meeting potential networking partners as well.

Practice Listening

The best way to practice listening is to stop talking. Other people don't like silence and will normally fill it up with increasingly more open and personal conversation if you let them. Once this has begun, you can encourage them to continue. If you show interest in the conversation, you will learn a lot and gain the trust of the other person.

Chapter 12

Always Set Your Priorities

The only job that I was ever fired from was as a waiter in Norman, Oklahoma. I had twelve years of restaurant experience and had taken the job to earn extra money while finishing up my PhD at the University of Oklahoma. I went through the typical training session and then showed up promptly for my first shift. I worked the whole first week without hearing of any problems, but at the end of the week, the manager said it wasn't going to work out and abruptly fired me. At first, I was embarrassed and shocked. I knew how to be a good waiter, and my previous work proved it. How dare they fire me without even giving a reason? When I went back to pick up my paycheck, I scheduled a meeting with the manager and asked what had happened. "Your heart just wasn't in this job," she said. "We hire experienced waiters here because we want them to really concentrate on this job and give our customers the best service in town. It is clear that your priorities are with finishing graduate school, not waiting tables." As it turned out, she was exactly right. I began teaching classes for the university to make money and build experience and took out a loan to make up the extra money needed for living expenses for my final year of graduate school.

We have probably all heard the phrase "That person really has their priorities straight." Have you ever written your priorities down? Priorities are simply a way of organizing things in top-to-bottom order. For most people, maintaining their personal health and supporting their family is at the top of the list. A career is most often second on this list, followed by all the other things that we do in ranked order. Setting up a planner was discussed in the "Organization" chapter, so we won't go through those details again, but we need to discuss the framework for setting priorities in the near term, medium term, and long term.

Unwritten Rules of Chapter 12

Use the one-more-thing approach.

Doing today's required work may be enough to keep your job, but it doesn't do anything to work toward medium- and long-term personal goals. Pick one more thing to do each day that moves you toward your personal and professional goals.

Stay in the Now until Today's Work Is Done

One of the most difficult things related to priorities is to make progress on them each and every day. There are so many potential distractions: friends, the Internet, family, pets, television, video games, etc. Cell phones and computers can be the worst. It is so easy to call and text and e-mail and surf the web that many people spend their day at work doing these things. Surprisingly, most of these people will proudly tell you that they put in a hard day's work, but if you compare what they got done to a more focused employee, it is obvious that they have work to do on their short-term priorities. The armed forces like to say that they do more before 8:00 a.m. than the rest of us will do all day. If you think about it, this makes a lot of sense. They get up so early that there are almost no other distractions going on (not even sunlight). They are given a very specific single task to do, like run ten miles, and they are not allowed to even think about something else until this task is accomplished. They don't have to deal with children or pets or television or other things distracting them from their goals. They will be assigned free time and can catch up on personal things when their job is done. I am not suggesting that the military is the best model for all workers or businesses, but you have to admit that it does a great job of demanding that people get their short-term priorities accomplished before they can do anything else. If you arrive a little early to work, you might also be able to get more done. If you can attack the day's tasks without getting too distracted, your productivity will certainly go up.

Use the One-More-Thing Approach

In addition to prioritizing each day, it is important to feel like progress is being made toward medium—and long-term goals. My method for doing this is the one-more-thing approach. When I have completed the tasks that absolutely need to be done today, I do one more thing. That thing might be searching for lodging for a field trip or a vacation that is still a year away. The thing could also be calling a financial professional to set up a meeting about investments and retirement. Most often, it is a call or e-mail to a potential networking contact to help set up a future partnership. These are all valuable things to do, but they can seem too overwhelming to tackle on any given day. By assigning yourself the task of simply doing one per day, you can stay ahead of schedule for the middle—and long-term projects without compromising today's necessary work.

Do It Now!

Sometimes the one-more-thing approach doesn't make enough headway toward an important goal. If you are planning to change careers, for example, everything from researching the new career to taking classes may be necessary in order for you to make this change. A few years back, I talked to one young man who said he wanted to become an environmental engineer but was currently busy paying the bills by mowing lawns. He planned to save up money, get his degree, and then go into landscape architecture. I saw him again a couple of years later and received the same story. By this time, he had gotten married and started a family and was supporting them with the lawn-mowing service. He still had the dream of being a landscape architect but was no closer to achieving it. His argument was that by the time he made enough money to pay the bills, he was too tired, and the money was too low to allow him to continue his schooling. It is never too late to reach for your dreams, but the effort definitely seems to get harder the longer you wait. For that reason, it is very important to keep working toward them, no matter how slowly, so that you don't fall into the "I'll do it next year" trap.

Balance Career Goals with Family Goals

Family is usually at the top of the priority list, but many young people haven't really considered whether their career and family goals are compatible. I once had a young man proudly claim that he was not only going to be a prestigious lawyer but would also be a supportive spouse and a doting parent. He would never miss a little league game and would have a big family that would take big family vacations. These were all positive goals, but in most cases, reality would never let this combination happen. Lawyers typically work long hours (around sixty hours per week or more from some of the latest surveys). They are often on call and need to do research in addition to other work hours. If they wish to make partner, they don't take many vacations, and those who put family first are less likely to be promoted. If your goals don't match, something is going to fail.

Find Your Big Dream, then Go Get It

Would you like to own a bed-and-breakfast in Hawaii? Do you want to retire in Boulder, Colorado, so you can ski all winter and hike all summer? Are you excited about joining a mission group or nonprofit organization that does great things worldwide? Whatever your big dreams are, it is up to you to make them come true. Toby, one of my former students, got his start as an industrial photographer. He took pictures of the inner working of buildings and machinery. The pay was good enough to get by, but he wanted more. He had always dreamed of being a National Geographic—style photographer. He wanted exciting travel and to take pictures that highlighted the natural beauty of faraway people and places. Toby went back to school, getting degrees in geography and photography. Thanks to this hard work, he now has his own gallery. I was able to travel with him a few years ago to Bogotá, Colombia, and he took some pictures for me at the National Coffee Park (one of my favorite photos is one that Toby's wife took of the two of us standing next to Juan Valdez and his burro, the national symbols of Colombian coffee). Toby now owns an apartment in Atlanta and one in Bogotá, but he is still broadening his opportunities. He is currently training to become a registered nurse so that this additional skill will allow him to travel the world and build his photo portfolio.

Don't Sacrifice Your Ethics

It is great to reach your dream job or economic goals, but it is easiest to get there, and better on the conscience if good ethics are used along the way. Building the respect to get good references demands that you treat other people well even when you may be competing against them. Since the human network behind the scenes often determines your ultimate success, it is important to keep the following in mind.

1. Be authentic. Be open, honest, and accessible.
2. Admit mistakes. Most things can be fixed, but if you try to hide a problem or blame it on someone else, then the problem will turn back on you.
3. Always try to be a "present listener." Give others the attention that you would expect.
4. Follow up and follow through. Reinforce that you can get things done for others.

Each dream is unique, so each plan will need to be tailored to get there. The three things that are common for nearly all dreams are the need for money, specific skills, and the contacts that will help you get there. Saving money from day one of a career and working with a good financial consultant is a strong start. But what are you saving for? All three elements demand to know this before the rest can come together. A good financial consultant will let you know if your plans are realistic and will give concrete suggestions concerning the amount you will need to save to get there. Just like financial planning shouldn't wait for retirement, future contacts can't wait either. It is always a good time to be looking for advice from those who share a similar dream or especially from those who have successfully done what you wish to do. Seeking them out takes deliberate effort and may lead to many dead ends, but the result will be a plan that you are confident will be achievable, will be within your budget, and will meet your expectations.

Priority Quiz

		True	False
1.	Getting fired is the worst thing for your career.	———	———
2.	People who work early get more done than those who work late.	———	———
3.	It can wait until tomorrow.	———	———
4.	The military approach can teach valuable work skills.	———	———
5.	The one-more-thing approach can help medium-term goals.	———	———
6.	I will do it next year when I have the time.	———	———
7.	Career and family goals must be compatible for success.	———	———
8.	If I win the lottery, I will buy a retirement home in Hawaii.	———	———
9.	Only rich people need a financial consultant.	———	———
10.	The most important question regarding retirement is when.	———	———

Answers to the Priority Quiz

1. False. Getting fired from a job that is low on your priority list might actually be a good thing. It frees you to find another way to get the money you need and work on your professional goals now.

2. True. In my experience, many more successful people work ahead on projects and come in early to work. The people who stay late are usually running late because they haven't been using their time efficiently in the first place. They are tired and hungry and can easily get distracted by things such as spending time with their family or sleeping. In successful businesses, the boss usually arrives early and leaves early. There must be a good reason for this system.

3. False. There may be some things that need to wait until tomorrow, but if you fall into a pattern of thinking that things can wait until tomorrow, you will be in trouble. In only a few days, you may find it impossible to catch up.

4. True. The military system requires total attention to the task at hand and removes distractions that might hurt productivity. These skills can be used to help in any job.

5. True. If we simply do what it required each day, we never work toward medium—or long-term goals. Getting into the habit of doing one more thing, no matter how trivial, can make a huge difference in your quality of life.

6. False. If you don't keep working toward it now, you will probably never feel like you have the time. People fill up their time with important and unimportant things. The scariest thing about this is how fast life can pass you by. This is why so many people start again when their children graduate high school. Are you willing to wait up to twenty years to continue your personal goals? If not, then keep after them now.

7. True. Happy employees are more productive. Happy couples have reached an agreement about each of their roles in their marriage. If you understand what you want and need now, you will avoid a potential major problem later.

8. False. This is a cop-out because you know that the odds of winning the lottery are so low that there is no need to plan for it. This goal is possible simply by working and planning in that direction, but saying you will steadily work toward that goal for the next twenty-five years is a lot less sexy than hoping to hit it big by today with a lottery ticket.

9. False. Everyone needs financial advice. It can be received for free during tax season at libraries or universities. Financial consultants need to be researched like any other business, but their tax and earnings advice can help you build a plan and stay on track to achieve it.

10. False. It doesn't matter when you retire. What matters is that it is a transition to doing something you love to do. Some college faculty never retire. They are still teaching in their eighties because they love learning and interacting with people. Other people retire from the military or an industrial job in their early forties after twenty years of service and then start a whole different career for the love of it. Thanks to the modern financial system, retirement doesn't mean simply traveling, shopping, or playing golf while we collect a pension check. Most of us will be working through our sixties at least. If we are doing what we would like to do anyway and get paid for it, then we might as well call it the new retirement.

Review

1. Stay in the now until the day's work is done.

2. Use the one-more-thing approach. When your day's work is done, do one more thing to work ahead on medium—or long-term goals.

3. Do it now! Keep working on long-term goals, or before you know it, life will pass you by.

4. Balance career goals with family goals. Work hours and family hours must be in agreement between yourself and the needs of each member of your family. If these areas are not in balance, something is going to fall apart.

5. Find your big dream, then go get it! Big dreams don't hardly ever just land in your lap. You must identify them and work get there. If you put in the effort to pursue the dream, you will never have regrets of what might have been.

6. Don't sacrifice your ethics. Be open, honest, and trustworthy, and the personal benefits will pay off.

Self-Evaluation

Rate your priorities from 1 to 10. Explain your rating in the space provided.

Prioritizing skills   _____   _____

Have you set plans and goals for the short term, medium term, and long term?

Practice

It is certainly better to address this early before a career or a marriage is on the line. I encourage people to use the following list as a starting point to consider whether their spouse and career paths are matching up or if adjustments or compromises will need to be made.

1. I don't wish to get married, so my job will be the top priority. Career wise, these people have nearly total freedom. They can move overseas without worrying about a spouse or children's needs and are not distracted by the day-to-day needs of family life. The only concern with this choice may be if they feel lonely or unfulfilled later in life.
2. I wish to get married, but my career has to be the high priority. This individual may be a doctor, lawyer, architect, or business owner. They will make a lot of money and have the status that comes with it but need to have a spouse who is willing to support the family, the household, and any other things that this professional doesn't have the time or interest to do.
3. I wish to get married, and I will be just as happy supporting my spouse's career as my own. This is a cooperative attitude and the one where I eventually found myself fitting in the most accurately. I am happy to say that my wife has outearned me throughout the years. This was made possible in part because I was willing to do the additional parenting, housework, and other duties to support her longer hours and changing shifts. Our career and family needs have been able to work because I have

flexibility in my schedule to allow it, and neither of us is hung up on old-fashioned male/female stereotypes.

4. I am willing to go wherever I need to go to pursue my career. People with this attitude have a much-higher chance of success than those who will never leave their hometown or region due to family considerations. Promotions are often reserved for people who are willing to transfer to new locations, and education opportunities that are best for your career may only be found in a far-off location. If two people both want to spend their lives in one location, near their family, then they will certainly get by and have a good quality of life. The outwardly mobile, however, will almost always need to move in order to accomplish their professional goals.

5. I hope to spend _____ hours per week at work, _____ hours per week with my spouse/children, _____ hours per week on individual recreation, _____ hours per week with my friends/family.

6. In order to live comfortably, I will need to make _____ per year and live a lifestyle that has (circle one) modest income middle income upper middle income high income

If you, your partner, and your job all come to agreement on these points, you are on the way to avoiding some big conflicts and achieving a high quality of life.

Chapter 13

Politics: Get a Boost from Those Around You

The American dream goes something like this: A person with no resources comes to America. They get a job as a stockperson in the back of a grocery store. Through hard work, they not only buy the store, but they open a global chain of stores. This person goes from rags to riches in one generation and never looks back. Their children go to Ivy League colleges and become the next great doctors, lawyers, and politicians. I have heard, seen, and taught this story many times, and there is something missing from it. In addition to hard work, the people who become highly successful also have another key trait: they know how to utilize politics to their advantage. From getting a green card to setting up a financial plan to establishing credit to buy the first store, there are a lot of other people who had to assist the poor immigrant along the way. That includes treating each customer with respect because if the customers don't come back, the first store would go bankrupt immediately.

Unwritten Rules of Chapter 13:

Be the Light of Your Office

Your favorite person in the world is probably someone who has a positive attitude, at least when it comes to you. Being a consistently positive person is easier for some people than others, but it is possible and valuable for everyone. Why are so many successful people negative? It rubs off on all those around them, and especially early in a career, it can really hold them back. Who wants to work with a grump or someone who is always criticizing others? Negative people look for problems, not solutions. They make enemies, not friends. Be the positive influence in class or on the job and you will gain the friends who can help make things go more smoothly. Even better, you will enjoy what you are doing, which is the best reward of all.

Be Around and Be Visible When You Are Around

Getting your work done is a good start, but it isn't everything. In my first teaching job, my student evaluations were good, and I was accomplishing every task asked of me, but for some reason other people were getting promoted faster than me and getting research opportunities that I didn't even hear about. Why? They knew when to be around and how to stay in touch with the right people. No one ever told me about this, but I found out on my own one day. The dean had some funding for a project that was perfect for me, but someone else had gotten it. When I asked why I hadn't been considered, he said, "I came by your office, but you weren't around. It was a quick turnaround on this, so I found someone else to do it." From that point on, I realized that in any job, the boss has expectations of employees to be around and that opportunities are often missed because we haven't made it clear that we can be available and are looking for new opportunities in our work. The bottom line here is that not only do you need to be around, but you need to check in with the boss so that he/she knows when you are around. Let them know about good things and progress with your work, and you will be first in their mind when new opportunities or promotions come around.

The Secretary Is Your Friend

I have said this before, but you can't say it too many times. Support staff can be your greatest friend or most dangerous enemy in a workplace. Make them your friends, and you will hear about good and bad things in time to respond. Treat them disrespectfully, and life can get very difficult. Here are the basic guidelines:

Know the job description of the staff person and respect it. If they are supposed to make copies, give them your copies. Even this must be done properly, however. Copies take time so there should be plenty of time allowed for the work to fit into the staff person's busy day. Those people who get into the habit of rushing in late and saying, "I need this work right now" are being disrespectful to the staff person and to everyone else who got their work in on time, but now has to wait for the rush job to be completed.

Support the work style of the staff person. Some people are very efficient. Their desk is perfect, they have a system, and they don't want you messing it up or wasting their time with idle talk. If you make a request of this person, they expect you to have done all the appropriate research and have the request in order and approved before it is given to them.

Other secretaries are more social. They get bored staring at the computer and find it refreshing to have a little casual conversation throughout the day. They don't mind doing some follow-up work to help put a project together and will volunteer to help given the chance. It is up to you to find out which type of person works with you and to make their day easier by matching your style to their needs. Whatever the work style of the staff person is, be sure to keep the relationship professional. Becoming too casual can lead to misunderstandings with the staff person, with other staff, and with other office workers.

Don't Be a Brownnoser

There is a big difference between working hard and being politically savvy and being a brownnoser. The person involved can't always see this difference, but everyone around them certainly can. Following the boss around too much is one example. Giving false praise to people in higher positions is another sign of brownnosing. Finally, being willing to serve as a mole or tattletale about the activities of peers is a sure sign of trouble. In each case, this type of behavior is disrespectful of other people's time and can be downright unethical in the chase for personal advancement. Supervisors usually don't like or respect the brownnoser either, but they will use them to accomplish their own goals. Ultimately, the supervisor will usually promote someone they respect for work ethic and accomplishments over the brownnoser and will write a poor reference letter for the brownnoser when they are looking for another job.

Hitch Your Wagon to the Right Horse

Consider that your wagon is your career, and the horse is a person who can help you get there. In most cases, you get to choose where you work or who you utilize as a mentor in the place that you do work. These people can be supportive and help tow your wagon toward the promised land, or they can rear up against you and send you and your wagon teetering off the trail and crashing into a ravine. The best mentors often have a lot in common with their protégé. They see you as a younger version of themselves; they are willing to give great advice and offer opportunities to help you get to where you want to go. This makes it important to befriend someone who is in a position that you respect, and if at all possible, pick someone who has the exact job that you would like to have someday. I have been on both sides of this process. During my master's degree, I simply stuck with the research advisor that the university assigned to me. We were not a good match. In the end, my wagon crashed, and only an intervention with a helpful secretary and a supportive graduate committee allowed me to survive the experience and earn my degree. My PhD experience was just the opposite. I visited with all the faculty in my new department this time and selected the one who was most interested in my research direction and who had a similar set of values. Not only did my graduate work sail smoothly this time, but this mentor became a lifelong friend and advisor who deserves a lot of credit for my professional success.

What You Say to Your Peers Can Be Held Against You

We spend a lot of time competing against our peers. Whether it is in sports or the classroom, this is a habit that is hard to break. In the real world, we do have to compete with peers for jobs and promotions, but on a daily basis, we are much more likely to be dependent on our peers than to compete against them. Consider this: You are in the same boat with your peers for your whole life. Some of your peers will become very successful and may be in a position to help you later in life. Other peers have great skills of research or networking and would be great people to share information with related to job opportunities. Still other peers may have strong connections with the boss and may be in a position to help or hurt you that way. For all of these reasons, it is good to avoid conflicts. Make it a policy never to volunteer negative comments and to offer compliments whenever they are warranted to build a positive reputation with peers. This way, when a peer hears about a job that is not right for them but may be perfect for you, they will give you a call.

Be the Light of the Office

My father began his professional career at IBM in the 1960s. He wore the classic business outfit of the day: navy suit, pressed white shirt, tie, and shined wing-tip dress shoes. Everyone looked the same. Everyone received the same training, but somehow, certain people became much more successful than others. Most of them were working hard, that was not a secret, so what made the difference? One element was attitude. My father decided early on that he was always going to have a positive attitude in the office. His standard reply in the morning to someone saying, "How are you today, Jim?" was "Just about the greatest!" Imagine the difference that this conveys than a simple "okay" or even worse: "Well, I'm not that great. I didn't sleep well, and I am behind on my paperwork." People may ask how you are doing, but it is a courtesy only. They don't really want to know about anything negative in your life unless it directly affects your work performance. People are much more interested in their own needs. In addition to saying "Just about the greatest!" my father would follow up with "How are you today?"

Thanks to my father's response being positive, the other person would normally respond in the positive as well. Regardless of their response, he would listen thoughtfully to the end. Being positive all the time is hard work, but it really pays off. If you are a positive influence, your peers and your boss will look forward to talking with you. They will know that something good is about to happen, something is about to get done, or a compliment will be on the way.

After he finished with IBM, my father and mother went on the road and played music in nightclubs up to six nights per week for twenty years. Being positive was even more important here. Can you imagine going out to listen to music and seeing people who were not smiling, didn't interact with the crowd, or acted depressed all evening? Certainly bad things happened on many work nights, but whether they were healthy, sick, sad, or angry, my parents knew the show had to be positive. Amazingly, when they put on that brave face and smiled and acted happy for a few hours, it often really did improve their mood and help them get over whatever was bothering them. Being positive can get you out of a funk and keep it from rubbing off on others. Remember, "the show must go on."

Know When and How to Say No

I used to be a habitual yes-man. For one thing, I have a tendency to want to please people, and saying yes usually makes people happy. In addition, years of graduate school and pretenure college teaching trained me to fear that if I ever said no to someone, my graduate career or teaching career might be over.

As it turned out, this extreme view is not correct. In fact, saying yes to everything not only weakens your political standing, it often leads to your getting stretched way too thin, and then the quality of work suffers. It is important to say no sometimes, such as when a boss you worked for part-time says you need to work overtime all week and that also happens to be finals week in college.

When do you say no?

1. When the request will stretch you too thin and the quality of your most important work will suffer
2. When a yes will put your ethics in question
3. When the person asking you really has the responsibility to do the work themselves
4. When there is no financial or political benefit that can come of this extra work
5. When the request might lead to a problem for your family
6. When the request will hurt your long-term balance of work and fun time

Once you have established that you are willing to say no when it is appropriate, a proper method must be used. It is important to keep it simple and honest. Most times, no is enough. If nothing else is asked, don't volunteer it. If more is needed, keep it to a minimum. If you don't want to work overtime because you have tickets to a concert, say something like "I can't work that night because I have a prior commitment." You don't need to volunteer more and shouldn't back down or try to justify your personal life. If you do back down or give long explanations, the other party will feel confident that they can back you down, not only this time but in the future when the same situation comes up. As long as you are around when you need to be and are known for doing high-quality work, you will be respected for saying no, and it will greatly improve your quality of life.

Politics Quiz

		True	False
1.	Politics is a big part of the American dream.	____	____
2.	The secretary can help you get your next job.	____	____
3.	Working behind hurts an entire office.	____	____
4.	Brownnosing is usually synonymous with breach of ethics.	____	____
5.	Loyalty is most important: stick with assigned mentors.	____	____
6.	Peers may be the key to getting your dream job.	____	____
7.	Being positive is good for your employment health.	____	____
8.	It is OK to say no to the boss.	____	____
9.	Always give a full explanation when you say no.	____	____
10.	Beware of people who are too nice.	____	____

Answers to the Politics Quiz

1. True. Someone needs to approve nearly everything we ever do. Whether it is the person who approves a small business loan or someone who gives us the first great job, we must provide the political atmosphere to make that person's answer be yes.

2. True. I once had a very respected faculty member volunteer to write reference letters for me. I was thrilled and immediately requested a letter for a job that I had applied for. A week later, the secretary of the office pulled me aside and said, "I don't know why, but Professor—wrote a very negative letter for you. I wanted you to know so that you wouldn't use him again." I didn't even get an interview for the first job with the bad reference, but I never used him again. I am still not sure why he would volunteer and then write a negative letter, but if it hadn't been for a thoughtful secretary, this person might have singlehandedly kept me from ever getting an academic job.

3. True. When you work behind and then need other people to drop what they are doing to get something done at the last minute, it is disrespectful to everyone. It is going to happen to everyone occasionally, but if it is a regular pattern, people will resent you.

4. True. Brownnosing is no laughing matter. Those who give false praise or talk badly about their peers may seem to be benefitting from this behavior in the short term, but in the long run, they will pay heavily for this behavior.

5. False. There are times when loyalty is important, but if a work mentor or college advisor is not helping you or you don't like them, it is time for a change. This is not just a matter of comfort. A great mentor can help set you up for life, and a bad mentor can send your wagon crashing into a ditch.

6. True. Social networking with peers is one of the best ways to find out about jobs these days. There may be times when you are

competing directly with them, but more often, you will benefit from the shared resources and experiences of your peers in the job market.

7. True. Not only is being positive good for your employment health, it is good for your physical health as well. Laughter is physically good for you, and making a positive attitude into a work habit will be good for you and uplifting for those who work with you.

8. True. Saying no, when it is appropriate, establishes limits that will be respected by the boss. The boss wants you to maximize productivity for the long term. With that in mind, saying no to things that would hurt your quality of work or stunt your professional development is perfectly acceptable.

9. False. People don't want or need the full story behind a no. Giving a long explanation weakens your position, so keep any answer simple and firm.

10. True. Why are some people so nice? Sometimes it is because they are legitimately nice and helpful people. Other times, they are working an angle that may not be helpful to you at all. If someone is unusually nice, be careful. Don't be rude, but try to figure out if they have some personal or political agenda that can be served by their allying with you or volunteering to help you with work (if you have established trust with the secretary, this might be a good question to ask them).

Review

1. Be around and be visible when you are around. Good things happen to those who are in the right place at the right time. Find out when that time is for your boss and your peers, and be there.

2. The secretary is your friend. They know everyone, they know everything, they can make good or bad things happen to you, so take good care of them.

3. Don't be a brownnoser. It may seem like a good strategy in the short run to give false flattery to others, but in the long run, they won't respect you, and your peers won't respect you either.

4. Hitch your wagon to the right horse. Choose mentors and reference writers carefully. If you use the right people, your professional ride will go much faster and more smoothly.

5. Be the light of the office. A positive attitude is infectious. It will bring smiles and opportunities your way.

6. Know when and how to say no. No one can do everything. People will test you to the limit, but only you can determine how much work is too much. If the quality begins to suffer, something must be let go.

Self-Evaluation

Rate your political skills from 1 to 10. Explain your rating in the space provided.

Politics   _____   _____

How well do you work with and work for the people around you? Do they know who you are and want to help you?

Practice

How do you practice politics if you are not a politician? We are all politicians to a certain extent. We are trying to get things done, and we need other people to agree, help us, and approve those things. The best way to practice is to maintain a positive attitude and to consider these questions each time you need to ask for something:

- How will my request be a good thing for the colleague or supervisor I am asking?
- Can I phrase this request so that it shows I am helping accomplish goals that are important to them?
- Have I done enough research to know what I am asking and everyone who will need to be involved to see this thing through?
- If the other person will need to do some work to support me, do I have an offer to help them with one of their goals as a payment for this assistance?

If you can answer yes to the questions above, you will be well on your way to making good political connections that will serve you now and in the future.

Chapter 14

Make Time for Fun!

We have spent the majority of our time discussing how to work smarter, get organized, make the right contacts, and be efficient with your time. These are all important tasks, but there is another important aspect of productivity that is not advertised: taking and using your free time the right way. Think of the simple ant. It hatches, works, sleeps, and dies. Many people get caught up in this same cycle. The only priority is work, and they fit in eating, sleeping, and other activities around their work schedule. They have reduced all their individual potential to the same lifestyle as an ant. When will they take the time to have fun? Fun doesn't schedule itself into your life. It has to be purposely included. In my mind, human life is an amazing blessing. Our self-awareness gives us the opportunity to enjoy life to the fullest, and we have an obligation to take full advantage of this. When we have our free time, we can enjoy love, creativity, personal fitness, and laughter in our lives. The ant may not need these things, but a healthy person does. How is this professionally useful? If you don't make time for fun, very unproductive things like depression, illness, and burnout are likely to creep into your life and ruin any gains in productivity that you think you are getting by skipping fun time.

Unwritten Rules of Chapter 14:

Have Your Fun

The boss might say, "You're going on vacation? We have lots of things here that need your immediate attention." But in reality, the boss doesn't want a burned-out employee who is out of ideas and frustrated at work.

A college advisor may say, "Take twenty-one hours of classes this semester, and you will stay ahead of schedule to graduate." But a college doesn't want a bunch of overworked, underachieving students. They want energized, excited students who are preparing for a career. Take your time off and enjoy it. It will improve your attitude and improve your productivity. As long as you keep your medium—and long-term priorities on track, you should have all the fun you can. That is the best reward for putting in the time to set up your life the right way in the first place.

Make Your Life Sustainable

As an environmental studies professor, I have seen the research pendulum swing in my career from a focus on cleaning up past mistakes to creating a sustainable plan of resource management. This means that the way we produce things doesn't use up our natural resources or cause any lasting damage for the future. With regard to raw material use, waste products, and pollution, sustainability has become the goal of business and environmental professionals. How does this relate to your free time? The same concept of sustainability should be incorporated into your personal life. Your energy and effort at work are a resource. You can get overused at work just like soil can get overused by a farmer. The result is the same in each case: lost productivity.

Find Your Balance of Work and Fun

Is your life in balance with regard to work and fun? One of the categories in the overall survey of professional development is extracurricular activities. I often have students who rate themselves a 10 in this category but then reduce this number after our interview. The most obvious people out of balance are college students who spend all their time partying and very little on their schoolwork. The teeter-totter of their activities is too heavily weighted on the fun side. Other students are working too hard. In the space, they list that they are members of the student government association, are part of a sorority or fraternity, are on the college swim team, carry an overload of classes, have a part-time job on the side, etc. They believe that the more activities they have, the higher their rating in this category. When asked about this, most modern students say that they have the opportunity to do so many things, that they are stretched too thin, and that they get stressed. Their teeter-totter has all the weight on the work side of the balancing point. If extracurricular activities cease to be fun and become simply another job for which you don't get paid, it is probably better to drop them. Each person has a different tolerance for the number of activities they can simultaneously juggle. If you feel overworked, tired, or depressed for more than just a passing week or two, it is probably time to reevaluate your nonwork responsibilities and cut back on some of them. Just like a teeter-totter, your life is only a fun ride when the different sides are in balance.

Stay in Shape for a Mental Edge

One of the first things that people drop after high school is physical fitness. The freshman's ten-pound gain is a common response to partying more and exercising less. One of the biggest excuses that I hear is "I don't have time to work out because I need to study." This argument is wrong for two reasons:

1. Meaningful exercise can be accomplished in about thirty minutes per day.
2. The mind's own productivity is going to diminish the longer you stare at the same materials.

This means that people who break up their studying into several sessions of two hours or less with some exercise (even a twenty-minute walk) in between will maintain a higher productivity level than someone who tries to work straight through without a break for six hours or more.

Stay in Shape for a Physical edge

My college recently started offering Fitness for Life program for all employees. It is voluntary and is offered free to anyone who wants to participate. Several times per week, people can join organized exercises ranging from yoga to cycling. They also receive instruction on healthy eating and other aspects of staying fit. Why would a business offer its employees this benefit for free? It's really not free. Research has shown a direct correlation to people using these programs and increased productivity. If they are more physically fit, they are less likely to lose time due to sick days or to suffer from depression or other mental issues. This helps save money in the short term and the long term for the business.

Build the Right Quality of Life

One of the building blocks of the American dream is the vacation. Industrial revolution—era America worked its employees up to six days per week and up to twelve hours per day. People tolerated this all year and anxiously awaited their two-week paid vacation. They used this time to travel to exotic destinations and visit friends and family. These days, many people are not taking two weeks straight or more for vacation. Some businesses even let you save up unused vacation hours for years and then pay you for them when you retire. Don't fall for this trap. A sustainable work plan should include plenty of time off for personal recreation and extended family time. If the work gives you vacation hours, take them. If they don't have official vacation hours, find a way to arrange your time off into meaningful chunks of time. This will allow you to fully relax, avoid the guilt of relationship duties that have been neglected, or do something exciting and meaningful for yourself. If you take enough time off to become refreshed, then your productivity will be higher when you return to work.

Build Fun into Your Work Schedule

One of the greatest things about a professor's job is the flexibility. I am not required to teach over winter break or summer break, but I often do it anyway. This may sound contrary to the previous section about taking all opportunities for time off, but this is different. When I teach in the winter term, it is usually to offer a field class to Hawaii or some other tropical location. Being in Hawaii in January is much more pleasant than being in Missouri in January, and since I control the agenda of the class, the research focus is on things that I am excited to see and learn for my own professional development. Summer teaching has included several field trips to Greece and a summer floating in rivers in the Ozarks region with teachers while working for National Geographic Society. All of these activities are work, but they are fun and exciting as well.

Take Control of Your Job Possibilities

While many jobs don't offer you exciting work options, almost any career is going to allow some flexibility in designing your job description and pursuing professional development opportunities. Taking advantage of a seminar on leadership is one example. Many businesses will pay all or part of this type of activity, and there are some very exciting destinations where these conferences take place. The only limit here is your own imagination. I know an auto mechanic who spent a summer in Germany doing auto training. There are chefs who work in new restaurants all over the world, K-12 teachers who spend a year teaching English in Japan or China, and police officers who go to Paris to learn new techniques in police work. The only trick is that no one can put this plan together for you. Only you know what extra work will be fun and beneficial and how it can fit into your life. Once you decide on something you want to do, pursue it diligently. It might take a few years to put it together, but the benefits can help your attitude and your career for a lifetime.

Don't Wait to Retire to Start Having Fun

Many people justify working for years without vacation by saying they will get to retire early. Here is one reason why this might not be a good strategy. You can't know that you and your spouse will be physically and mentally healthy enough to do all the great things you have planned when you reach sixty-five years old. My parents didn't buy into the delayed gratification at all. One year, in their early thirties, they planned to work six nights a week for the whole year and save all the money they could. They took their savings and rented a house in Guadalajara, Mexico, for the year. For that entire year, they played with their children (I was two years old at the time), played music, swam, surfed, and visited with friends. Can you imagine how great a year like that could be? Most Americans don't even take a continuous month off in their career, while Europeans do this every year. While many friends told my parents they were wasting retirement money, they chose to live that experience. Years later and well before retirement age, my mother became ill and passed away. If they had waited to start having fun, they would have never had the opportunity. In the end, work and responsibility are always going to be important, but a balance of fun is what makes it all worthwhile.

Balance of Work and Fun Quiz

		True	False
1.	The more extracurricular activities you have, the better.	_____	_____
2.	Working harder always pays off.	_____	_____
3.	Fitness for Life Program helps your productivity.	_____	_____
4.	Having fun is more important than work.	_____	_____
5.	It takes a lot of time to stay in shape.	_____	_____
6.	Flexibility is possible in most jobs.	_____	_____
7.	Sometimes more work is fun.	_____	_____
8.	It is worth saving vacation hours for retirement.	_____	_____
9.	Vacations should be taken in big blocks if possible.	_____	_____
10.	The most productive workers make their work fun.	_____	_____

Answers to the Balance of Work and Fun Quiz

1. False. Too many extracurricular activities can weigh you down. If they feel simply like unpaid work, then something has to go.

2. False. Working hard is a good goal, but working steadily and efficiently is a better one. People often feel that the more hours they work, the better. Unfortunately, productivity drops off without proper breaks and distractions, so all that extra time might be wasted time.

3. True. Exercise and good eating habits reinforced at work have been shown to increase alertness and decrease sick days. Take advantage of these programs if they are offered, and if not, find a friend who will serve a similar purpose of adding peer pressure to an exercise and healthy eating program.

4. False. Being unemployed is not very fun. Having fun is important, but it must be balanced with quality work so that you can pay the bills and advance as a professional.

5. False. Staying in shape takes about thirty minutes per day of rigorous activity, in addition to eating a healthy diet. Anyone can do this. The key is to pick something that will be enjoyable, or the interest will fade over time, and bad habits will return.

6. True. Almost any job has options, but they aren't advertised. In many cases, other employees or supervisors haven't even considered the options. It is up to you to decide what you would like to do and develop a proposal on how to get there. Some businesses are going to a four-to-ten hour shift a week with three days off. The supervisors hope to get more productivity out of the four days, and the employees are hoping to get more refreshed with three straight days off.

7. True. If extra work is of your own choice and especially if it puts you together with an exciting place or interesting people,

then you are basically getting a paid vacation. Look for these opportunities, but be sure that you don't do so many of them that they tip the balance to the work side too much and lead to burnout.

8. False. Are you willing to wait to have fun until retirement? There is no guarantee that you will be healthy enough to enjoy retirement anyway. Have fun now, and you will avoid the guilt of missing out on family fun or the pain of failing to live up to personal dreams and goals.

9. True. Faculty have to wait six years to earn a really big block of time for rejuvenation (sabbatical), but then we get up to a whole school year off to pursue our own goals. What a luxury. This allows for time to be creative, have fun, catch up on private matters, and really connect to friends and family. Universities have discovered that a big block of time for vacation leads to faculty returning refreshed and full of creative new ideas and energy. Most jobs make it difficult to take off more than two weeks at a time, but it is my opinion that you should take off the biggest block you can, rather than take off an extra day here and there. Quality of life ratings are higher in Europe than the US related to work/family time. One significant factor in this is that most Europeans take off a full month in the summer and do their traveling and socializing then. Give this a try, and see if it works for you.

10. True. How we feel at work is controlled the most by our own attitude. I have known janitors who came to work singing every day and looked forward to talking to people in the bathroom or hallway as they worked. I have also seen high-level administrators who spent their day complaining about their job, their employees, and everything else. Which type of person are you going to be? If you look good, you will probably feel good, and that can lead to a lasting positive attitude at work. I guarantee that this positive attitude will relate to higher productivity and, even more importantly, will make work more satisfying for the long run.

Review

1. Find your balance of work and fun. People who love their job never work a day in their life. Most of us need recreation to balance out the stress or boredom of work.

2. Stay in shape for a mental edge. Concentration is better if you feel better. Exercise reduces stress and releases healthy endorphins. Add an exercise regimen to your life and stick with it.

3. Stay in shape for a physical edge. More fit people have fewer sick days and thus have higher productivity. Do Fitness for Life if it is offered.

4. Build the right quality of life. Take your vacations. Have your fun. Don't save it up. You are not an ant, and people need their free time and their social time.

5. Build fun into your work schedule. One of the most important qualities of a dream job should be that it is fun for you to do. If your current job isn't fun at all, try to be creative about how to find some additional responsibilities, training seminars, or travel that will add fun and excitement to the job.

6. Take control of your job possibilities. One of my friends is fond of saying "everything's negotiable." Your role at work is one of those things. There is often more flexibility than you think, and even if it doesn't work out at one place, the experience you gain will probably help you find a job that better suits your lifestyle.

7. Don't wait to retire to start having fun. Fun is one of the best reasons to live. It makes you healthier, happier, and more productive. Once you are financially stable, I recommend that you use all the vacation time you have earned. Don't feel guilty; you have earned it!

Self-Evaluation

Rate your balance of work and fun from 1 to 10. Explain your rating in the space provided.

Extracurricular activities   _____   _____

Does your life have the right balance of work and fun? If not, then you are not on a sustainable path toward a high-quality life experience.

Practice

If you need to practice having fun, then this book was really a necessary investment. I am not talking about vacation time because most people know what to do with this time. It is a standard week that often gets people into a rut. The best possible situation is if your work is fun. Chart out a normal work week on paper. How many hours at work were fun? How many hours weren't fun? How many hours of your personal time were fun? How many hours weren't fun? Consider the balance of work and fun, and make adjustments that help you realize the quality of life you want.

Professionalism Rating
Comments/Suggestions

Self-Evaluation

You have now completed the self-evaluation categories in each chapter. In order to score them and for other people to evaluate you, these categories are all in one place below.

Don't fill them in on the following pages. Make a copy of the page to fill out, and keep it as a record so that you can compare your progress over time. It is also recommended that you make a copy of the blank form and have a trusted friend or mentor fill it out for you. Please explain to them that you need truly honest feedback so they won't sugarcoat any weak areas.

Please use the following evaluation tool to rate your own professional development.

Professional Development Self-Evaluation

Name _____
Developed by Dr. Sean Terry

Rate each category from 0 to 10 with 10 being the best rating. Consider this to be like a grade, so a 9-10 is an A, 8 is a B, 7 is a C, 6 is a D, and anything below 6 is an F.

Be sure to add brief comments to justify why you chose this number to rate your ability in this category.

Impression

1. Attitude   _____ _____

First impressions can make all the difference. What positive traits can you convey in an interview setting? Can you show confidence without being arrogant?

2. Appearance   _____ _____

Do your hair, clothing, shoes, and personal hygiene make you a good match for the place you want to go? Some places want creativity to show, while others are very old-fashioned.

3. Punctuality   _____ _____

The comedian Woody Allen once said 90 percent of life is just showing up. How good are you at this?

4. Self-motivation   _____ _____

Where are you going, and how hard are you working to get there?

Networking/Business Success Strategies

5. Organization   _____ _____

From keeping on track daily to working steadily toward personal and private goals, organization is a big key to success at getting things done.

6. Asking for help   _____ _____

You don't want to be a pest, but asking questions shows respect to a professor or boss and allows you to efficiently use your time to complete projects the right way.

Don't be too shy or too stubborn to ask questions.

7. Group-working skills   _____ _____

How well do you lead, follow, trust, and delegate in a group-working environment? It is the only way to have productive long-term work relationships.

8. Team chemistry   _____ _____

Rate yourself on the ability to support good team chemistry at work or school

9. Networking contacts   _____ _____

Who do you know? Family, friends, church, peers, career center, alumni center, former supervisors, fraternity/sorority, faculty, intern, or job contacts—all need to be kept in contact to help you achieve your professional goals.

10. Adaptability   _____ _____

When faced with a no or other obstacle, how good is your strategy to adapt, change directions, or overcome?

Writing and Speaking

Whether it is an effective e-mail, application, or grant proposal, every job requires good writing. To be hired or to make a presentation, good speaking skills are required as well.

11. Overall quality   _____ _____

12. Research skills   _____ _____

13. Analysis skills   _____ _____

14. E-communication _____ _____

How effectively do you use e-mail and social media?

Critical Thinking

15. Creativity   _____   _____

Thought "I have a new idea for that" or "I could have done that"? Everyone has the potential to be creative. What do you build into your life to relax, meet new people, or find inspiration? Art, music, recreational reading, and even hiking in nature can all ease the stress on the quantitative side of the brain and allow us to solve problems in new and creative ways.

16. Open to new ideas _____   _____

Are you a good listener? It not only helps you learn, but it also shows respect to others.

17. Use of logic   _____   _____

Do you make decisions based on logical assumptions or quick, emotional responses? How effectively can you explain your logic to others?

18. Prioritizing skills _____   _____

Have you set plans and goals for the short term, medium term, and long term?

19. Politics   _____   _____

How well do you work with and work for the people around you? Do they know who you are and want to help you?

20. Extracurricular activities _____   _____

Does your life have the right balance of work and fun? If not, then you are not on a sustainable path toward a high-quality life experience.

Twenty categories. Two hundred points. Your percent is calculated by adding up your total and then dividing your total by 200 or by simply dividing the total points by 2.

Total points _____ Percent _____

Before you consider this a final score, sit down with someone you trust and go over your self-rating with them. Ask them to be honest in their evaluation of each category with regard to your performance. If there is a big difference between the two opinions, find a compromise for each category that is different and recalculate your total.

If your score was a perfect 200, you are living in a dream world. No one is perfect. Have someone close to you fill out the categories for you and then go over them again.

If your total score is above 180 (90 percent) and each individual category is a 7 or above, keep up the good work; you are on the right track.

Even though 7 is considered acceptable, clearly there is still room for improvement for ratings of 7 or 8. For these categories, conscious effort should be put into this category to improve it.

Any category that rates a 6 or below shows a serious deficiency. Go back to those sections in the book and follow the advice given to work on this area. Put real effort toward strengthening the professional development area, and in six months or less, you should see real progress.

Afterword

Congratulations on finishing the *Unwritten Rules* ! Please remember that improvement is not instant but takes practice. It is best to revisit the book once a year to check your progress. If you are changing academic settings or looking for a new job, that would also be a good time to revisit the themes of the book. I hope that this tool helps you achieve your personal and professional goals. If you have a positive story to share about using this resource or have suggestions to make it more useful, please contact the publisher online, through Facebook or Twitter.

Sincerely,

Sean Terry

Network Contact Reference Sheet

Name _____

Business _____

Date First Met _____

Most Recent Contact Date _____

Phone Number _____

Fax Number _____

E-mail Address _____

Website Address or Other Contact Information _____

Experience or Connections That This Reference Can Provide

_____

_____

_____

Friends or Other Colleagues of This Contact That Can Be Utilized As Well

---

Times and Dates That This Contact Has Been Used for Job Reference or Reference Letter

---

Request a Reference the Right Way

When you request for a reference letter, there are some rules to follow. First, you need to write a cover letter that politely asks for the reference and explains why you are applying for this position. It should briefly explain why you feel this person's reference letter will help you get the position. The cover letter should never be longer than one page. Then you need to provide the person whom you want to write the letter with the following:

1. Title of the position for which you are applying
2. Name and title of the person or committee to whom the letter is to be addressed
3. Full and exact address for the letter and a completed, addressed, and stamped envelope
4. Deadline by which the letter needs to be sent, giving the person all possible notice
5. A current résumé that includes all experience that you have that the person can utilize to help write a stronger letter

If you haven't seen the reference letter writer in a while, remind them of the work that you did for them and why this was a valuable experience for you.

E-mail, call, or even better, go by in person to make sure they have received the request.

Upon confirmation of the submission of the letter, write a thank-you note.

About the Author

Dr. Sean Terry is a professor of geography and environmental studies at Drury University in Springfield, Missouri. Dr. Terry has interviewed more than a thousand students, business professionals, career center employees, administrators, and teachers in his research on how to find and keep the right job. Dr. Terry had an unusual childhood, being part of a traveling family music show until he was sixteen years old. Professionally, he spent twelve years in the restaurant industry and served as the editor of the Missouri State University newspaper before receiving a PhD in environmental geography from the University of Oklahoma in 1995. Since then, he has worked as an environmental consultant and spent five years as the director of Missouri Geographic Education Foundation for National Geographic Society. Dr. Terry has advised hundreds of students to professional careers, graduate schools, scholarships, and fellowships. His academic specialties include field research of environmental problems in Hawaii, Greece, and the Ozarks of Missouri and Arkansas. He is also known as the food professor and has developed a reputation as an expert on world food and cuisine. Dr. Terry took an interest in professional development early in his own career and followed up on this seriously while working for National Geographic Society. This work led to the certification of hundreds of Missouri teachers with professional development credit in geography. The effort also led to a workbook publication titled *Geography Voyageur* that has been used by more than a million students in US classrooms to learn geography in a fun and interactive way. Dr. Terry has a wife and two children. He is currently working with his wife to set up a one-year work swap that would allow them to spend a year in Australia together as a family.

Index

CPSIA information can be obtained
at www.ICGtesting.com
Printed in the USA
FFHW020643090819
54184526-59890FF